T5-AOC-429

EYEWITNESS

Minnesota Voices on Climate Change

Compiled by Climate Generation: A Will Steger Legacy

Editors Jothsna Harris and Kira Liu

Copyright © 2020 Climate Generation: A Will Steger Legacy

All rights reserved. No part of this book may be reproduced or used in any manner without written permission of the copyright owner except for the use of quotations in a book review.

"Losing a Refuge" by Logan Reider was previously published as "Climate anxiety: the first step is the hardest" in *MinnPost* on July 26, 2019. "The Cradle of Our Youth" by Danny Friedman was previously published as "Danny's Climate Story" in *Grand Rapids Herald-Review* on November 17, 2019.

Book design by Bryn Bundlie

Editing by Betsy Barnum

Printed by Smart Set

ISBN: 978-173422982-0

PRINTED ON 100% POST CONSUMER WASTE RECYCLED PAPER

Published by Climate Generation: A Will Steger Legacy

www.climategen.org

Dedicated in hope and gratitude to the Climate Generation: everyone alive today who will solve the crisis of our time.

———————

Stories bypass rhetoric and pierce the heart. They offer a wash of images and emotion that returns us to our highest and deepest selves, where we remember what it means to be human, living in place with our neighbors.

```
-Terry Tempest Williams
```

EYEW

APPENDIX

Acknowledgments

While our climate stories are individual perspectives, it is important to emphasize that it is our collective voices that humanize the climate crisis and have the power to shift the narrative. *Eyewitness: Minnesota Voices on Climate Change* would not have been possible without the support of many contributors including a diverse range of voices, from prominent leaders to everyday residents, sharing their experiences of climate change. We gratefully acknowledge all Minnesotans who submitted works to this publication and who understand the urgency of using their voices to demand bold action on climate change from all levels of government and society.

With Special Thanks To:

The McKnight Foundation, who made this project possible with financial support.

Gratitude and respect for Selection Committee members who reviewed submissions, shared their expertise, and made recommendations with the greatest of consideration:

Ben Passer
Director of Energy Access and Equity at Fresh Energy

Erin Sharkey
Writer, producer, educator, and graphic designer, and co-founder of Free Black Dirt

Lisa Troutman
Illustrator, graphic recorder and owner of Drawn Well LLC

Mark Neužil
Professor of Journalism at the University of St. Thomas

Immense appreciation to all who contributed their talents to making a beautiful publication, including; Bryn Bundlie for design and layout, Betsy Barnum for editorial support, the team at Smart Set for printing, and with special guidance from James Lenfestey; all of whom understood the intention and helped to capture the spirit and importance of this book.

Curation by Climate Generation staff, including Jothsna Harris and Kira Liu, with tremendous support, cultivation and guidance from Nicole Rom, Kristen Poppleton, Sarah Goodspeed, and Lauren Boritzke Smith who were instrumental in the strategy of this project and keeping it grounded in the commitment to remain laser-focused on the beautiful and just future that we imagine is possible.

History of Project

There has never been a more important time to vocalize the ways we are experiencing climate change, through sharing our stories and our perspectives.

Building from polar explorer Will Steger's powerful first-hand accounts of climate change, *Eyewitness: Minnesota Voices on Climate Change* reflects the broad range of impacts and perspectives that speak to the depth and scope of how climate change is being seen and felt in Minnesota. This collection will be presented to policymakers as a piece of literary activism and testimony that bears witness to the personal relevance of our changing climate. *Eyewitness* has been collected from a mix of prominent leaders and residents of Minnesota about their experiences of climate change. It will be delivered with testimony to the Minnesota Legislature on the 50th anniversary of Earth Day in April 2020.

One of the most effective ways to engage people on climate change is to balance the science with the personal stories of how it is affecting us. Over the past several years Climate Generation has worked with hundreds of individuals to help cultivate and share personal stories of climate change as a key strategy to normalize conversations on climate change because, despite public opinion polls on climate change that show 70% of Americans understand that climate change is happening and that it will cause harm to future generations, yet two-thirds of Americans say they never talk about it. There are scores of divergent viewpoints in the media, misinformation is rampant, and science has become politicized. There is a disconnect between what people know and feel about climate change, and their willingness to talk with family and friends about it. Sharing our stories bridges this disconnect and gives us a way to influence our social construct, which shapes public opinion, in turn driving decision making by political representatives and business leaders.

This project is inspired by similar literary works of activism, such as *Testimony: Writers of the West Speak on Behalf of Utah Wilderness* and *Arctic Refuge: A Circle of Testimony*, which feature first-hand accounts as well as the work of prominent writers. Both works led to eventual victories in conservation efforts when presented and circulated in Congress.

Key Facts About Climate Change

Fact 1: Climate Change is Real

When we burn fossil fuels for energy, we add more and more carbon dioxide (CO2) into the atmosphere. This buildup acts like a blanket that traps heat around the world, which warms the atmosphere and oceans, disrupting the earth's climate system. Over 97% of climate scientists globally agree this is happening and that it is predominantly human-caused.

Fact 2: It's Happening Now

Climate change impacts all of us, but people of color and low-income communities bear a disproportionate share of the costs. In addition to an increase in global temperature, we are seeing changing patterns in precipitation, increasing humidity, changes in air pressure, and warming ocean waters. These impacts combined result in more frequent and intense extreme weather events, catastrophic flooding and fires, and unpredictable seasons that make food production less stable. To truly understand how climate change is affecting life across the world, we must balance the science of climate change with the personal stories of communities both devastated by the impacts and rising to introduce equitable solutions for a resilient future.

Fact 3: Humans Are Causing it

Climate change is fundamentally driven by our fossil fuel economy, which many have benefited from politically, socially, and economically. We are adding large amounts of greenhouse gases into the atmosphere through the burning of fossil fuels like coal, oil, and natural gas, which we use for energy, transportation, and powering our lives. Since the Industrial Revolution, we have been burning fossil fuels unsustainably, and it has resulted in a CO2 amount of 410 parts per million in our atmosphere – a level unprecedented in the last 5 million years. In Minnesota agriculture, including food production and land-use changes, also significantly contributes to climate change.

Fact 4: It's Urgent

The impacts of climate change are forcing communities to pay the price in many ways. Communities of color and low-income communities are disproportionately impacted by climate change because of systems of oppression. Extreme weather events are becoming increasingly common, the damage from which disrupts traditions, livelihoods, and compromises lives. Changes to Minnesota's natural systems are also increasingly clear; Minnesota's winters are warming faster than any other state in the nation, many of our keystone species are in peril, and Minnesota's water resources are threatened with an uncertain future.

Fact 5: We Have the Solutions

Action on climate change is happening all around us! We can come together and take action to drive decision-making that makes the sustainable choice the easy choice. We need everyone to do everything we can to urgently address climate change.

Collectively our response must match the scale and scope of the problem.

Ways To Take Action

Taking action on the climate crisis is critical, but knowing where to start can be overwhelming. We have a few simple suggestions to jumpstart your action journey using your voice, choice, and vote.

Use Your Voice

Sharing our personal stories of climate change can place facts into context and can help us understand how it is relevant to our lives. While climate stories are individual perspectives, it is our collective stories that have the power to shift the narrative. Everyone has a climate story, even if you don't know exactly what yours is. Think about your answer to the following prompts and weave together your climate story. If you're looking for ideas, coaching, or a place to share your story, drop us a line at stories@climategen.org

Story Prompt #1

Tell a personal story about an experience that helped shape the person you are today. How has that influenced the way you see the world?

Story Prompt #2

What is your experience of climate change? and/or
How have you been thinking about climate change lately?

Story Prompt #3

Tell a story about a time you felt resilient.

Story Prompt #4

What would a better world look like to you? What is the role that you will play in making it a reality?

Once you've developed your story, share it with others to build your confidence and refine it as you test it out. Tell it to a family member, neighbor, or colleague. Send it to your local paper as a letter to the editor, or send it to an elected official. Make sure your story includes an ask or an invitation to action!

Use Your Choice

The many choices we make every day have an impact on the planet and the people who live here. What should we eat? Should we fly, drive, walk, or take public transportation? What should we purchase new, purchase used, or choose not to purchase at all? Think about the choices you make every day, measure your carbon footprint, and commit to making better choices. Take those individual actions, tell other people about them, and scale it up for collective action. If you are composting in your home, can you encourage your neighbors to do it as well? Or your school? Or your faith community? Register to vote and then get out and register others!

Use Your Vote

Register to vote, educate yourself on candidates' records or intentions on climate action, and vote in every election for candidates who have climate-friendly policies and are willing to take significant action on climate. Candidates at all levels of government—from school board to the president—have the power to make important decisions that have an impact on climate change.

Write a letter to your elected officials

Dear ... (formal greeting using their title)

Introduce yourself – where are you from, what is your profession, school, or related background.

Tell them why you are writing (for example: I urge you to act on climate change).

Share your climate story – why do you care about climate change, what have you witnessed, how does this affect your district?

Connect with them in your story – we often remember stories more than facts, and relate to values on a personal level.

Move to action – what are solutions that they can influence in their position to build resilient communities?

Show gratitude – thank them for considering your words and share a common goal for your community and for the future.

Sincerely... (close with your name and legible address and contact information)

TNESS

Minnesota Voices on Climate Change

Table of Contents

Introduction

Tatanka Ohitika	B'dote	i
Nicole Rom	Foreword	iii-iv
Will Steger	Eyewitness to Climate Change	v-vii
Soni Shah and Kathleen Bacigalupi	We Are All Witnesses	viii-ix

Gratitude

Logan Reider	Losing A Refuge	1-3
David Coggins	Birch Woods	4
Kristin Maija Peterson	Basket	5-6
Danny Friedman	The Cradle of Our Youth	7-8
Kat Nottingham	Superior Sunrise	9-10
Brian Smoliak	Do You Sense It?	11-12
Kait Macheledt	On the Edge of Something Wild	13-14

Loss

DansAlux	Los Caminantes	17
Kristen Iverson Poppleton	The Work	18
Erika Gilsdorf	For the Love of Winter	19-20
Charles K. Dayton	The Loons Soon May Be Leaving; Minnesota Will Be Grieving	21-23
Marie Osuna	National Parks	24
Janet Malotky	Ascension	25-26
James Matthew Pipkin	A Future Memory of Cold	27-28
Julie Arnold	Everything is Connected	29-31
Rosella Joyce	Adieu	32
Lee Frelich	Climate Change in Northern Minnesota: Spruce, Maple or Savanna?	33-35
Kyle Bernier	Change	36
Mike Furtman	A Hunter's View	37-38

Responsibility

Mark W. Seeley	Seize the Day	41-43
Javier Elias Carrasco Miock	The Penitents	44

Michael Chaney	Misiziibi—Great River	45-46
Yordanose Solomone	The Currency of War	47-48
Rita Moe	Aboard the Pequod	49-50
Mike Menzel	All Persons Should Breathe Clean Air	51-52
Taji Joseph	Aftermath	53-54
Izzy Laderman	The Forgotten	55-56
Aaron "Lazerbeak" Mader	Waking Up	57-58
Dave Durenberger	The Choice	59-60
Marco A. Hernandez	Perspective From the Smokestack	61-63
James P. Lenfestey	I Carry the Grief of the World	64

Resilience

Ben Weaver	Disrupting the Binding	67-69
Katy Backes Kozhimannil	Bagosenim (Hope)	70
Jasmine Dawn Holt	Clearer Waters	71-72
Munira Berhe	Opening My Eyes	73-74
Akira Yano	Uncovering Rondo	75-77
Liz Lat	Bedtime Stories of the Khmer Americans	78-80
David Joel Riviera	Solid Spiral	81-82
Dani Pieratos	Breathe	83-84
Ricardo Levins Morales	Stop Global Warming	85-86
MaryBeth Hoover Garrigan	Family Stories of the Past Give Insight to the Future	87-88

Hope

Jeremy Messersmith	No Spoilers	91-93
Aajay Harris	Bridges	94
David A. Foster	Excerpts from Oral Testimony to the House Select Committee on the Climate Crisis	95
Robyne Robinson	Fireflies	96
Kao Kalia Yang	Essay on Delivery of My Boys	97-98
Lisa Troutman	When I am Feeling Overwhelmed	99-100
Arlene Birt	The (Potential) Speed of Change	101-102
Jay T. McCleary	Love and Loss: A Pond Hockey Story	103-105
Zaria Elisha Romero	Trash Talk	106-109
Chris Heeter	For the Earth Warriors...	110-112

Appendix

Acknowledgments	115-116
History of Project	117-118
Key Facts About Climate Change	119-120
Ways To Take Action	121-124
About Climate Generation	125

INTRODUCTION

Intention

Eyewitness: Minnesota Voices on Climate Change elevates the human experience of climate change through personal narrative and creative expression. It serves as a tool for facilitating conversations with local policymakers to inspire and strengthen their support for climate and clean energy solutions.

Local communities have a unique opportunity and potential to create an undercurrent of momentum toward climate solutions and reinforce efforts to address the climate crisis at the city, state and business levels, creating pathways to change that our national and global leaders cannot easily ignore. *Eyewitness* brings a local flavor to this complex challenge of our time through a place-based focus on impacts and solutions, and by elevating the diverse experiences and voices of Minnesotans. Our best hope for *Eyewitness* is that it will lead to major victories in ambitious local policies that strongly and equitably address climate change, sparking inspiration beyond Minnesota.

We invite you to consider your own climate story, wherever you are from, and to share it as you engage people in conversations in your community, with local decision makers, and beyond. This is a way that all of us can facilitate understanding and build urgency for why we must protect all people and all places.

B'dote
[ba-DOE-tay]

B'dote,
it is where the rivers meet,
it was that
before this place
was called,
Fort Snelling
this place
used to take us, Dakota
away from here.
B'dote,
it was here
before
Minnesota,
it is, where the waters come together,
it will remain,
B'dote
Forever,
No matter
What we say or do,
B'dote,
B'dote...

Tatanka Ohitika, Age 73
Saint Paul, MN
Poet / Dakota / Activist

We'd like to begin this book by acknowledging that Minnesota is part of the traditional, ancestral, and contemporary lands of the Dakota and Anishinaabe people—land stolen through misleading treaties in the 1800s. It is critical to acknowledge this, as the climate crisis is, in part, due to a disconnect from the land and the systems of oppression that shape the everyday experience of Indigenous individuals and communities. We recognize the tremendous resilience of Indigenous communities and their powerful leadership for climate solutions.

Foreword

By Nicole Rom
Executive Director
Climate Generation: A Will Steger Legacy

Minnesotans are experiencing the effects of climate change: from higher temperatures, to more extreme storms with intense flooding, to changes in our cherished ecosystems and four seasons. Indeed, Minnesota's winters are warming faster than winters in any other state. The cumulative effects of climate change are having real impacts on Minnesotans and our economy by forcing costly repairs to infrastructure, increasing home and crop insurance rates, contributing to upheaval in our native ecosystems, and causing more trips to the hospital for heat-related illnesses. Some communities are feeling the impacts of climate change more acutely than others, particularly low-income, Indigenous, and communities of color.

EYEWITNESS is a chapbook collection of prose, art, poetry and essays showing us who the truth-tellers are: scientists, artists, writers, poets, health care workers, entrepreneurs, Indigenous leaders, educators, farmers, gardeners, union workers, activists, parents and children. This book is more than a look at how climate change is already impacting Minnesotans. It is a collection of personal reflections based on science and first-hand experience, emphasizing that we are no more nor less than the relationships that sustain us. Without the relationships and landscapes that have shaped us and informed who we are, our home becomes unrecognizable.

EYEWITNESS is a testimony to these changes and a call for action to all, from everyday citizens to policymakers. In this era of climate change, we are being given an unprecedented opportunity to come together and embrace a transformational moment of courage, collective discipline, and devotion to survival. It is daunting. It is sobering. And it is essential. It can also be a time of immense creativity. What is at stake? Everything we hold dear from place to people to planet. This is a stellar moment. This is our calling. This book can serve as a guide.

EYEWITNESS is a collection of small acts: witnesses who are inspiring others and contributing to a momentum of change that can trigger the social determination we need. Stories, poems and art expose the truth, conveying powerful messages that tap into our emotions and can cut across barriers.

Let these pages be an awakening. Let this moment be a reckoning in which we realize there is no hope without action. And let our greatest actions be rooted in compassion for all species, not just our own.

Eyewitness to Climate Change

By Will Steger
National Geographic Explorer and Founder
Climate Generation: A Will Steger Legacy

I am an eyewitness to climate change: every ice shelf I have crossed by dogsled, foot or ski has disintegrated into the ocean.

Climate change is a reality. It threatens both our society and life as we know it on Earth. The overwhelming consensus of the scientific community for several decades has been that the planetary warming we are experiencing is largely a human-induced phenomenon.

The Arctic and the Antarctic regions have been my home for over 50 years. To survive in these lands, I have become intimately familiar with their vast landscapes, wildlife, and climates. The changes I see deeply affect me in a way neither a scientific study nor a satellite image could.

I have been to both poles numerous times, and I've seen catastrophic consequences caused by climate change. I crossed the Ward Hunt Ice Shelf in the Arctic and Larsen Ice Shelves on Antarctica. To the astonishment of scientists, the Larsen A and B ice shelves, which took my expedition team a month to cross by dogsled in 1989, abruptly collapsed into the sea in 1998 and 2002 respectively as a result of climate change. I experienced firsthand the melting of the sea ice on the Arctic Ocean. In March 2007, while on Baffin Island, just days after we crossed Cumberland Sound, the entire ice sheet broke up and was blown out to sea. If this had happened a day earlier or if the team traveled a day later, the situation could have been serious for us. For the local people who live and hunt around Cumberland Sound, the situation is serious; the poor ice conditions mean dangerous or impossible travel between outpost camps and the inability to fish and hunt for subsistence.

The Arctic sea ice in the northern hemisphere of our planet has lost over half of its thickness and area in the last few decades. It's once reflective surface is now exposing the darker surfaces of open water. Because darker surfaces absorb more energy than lighter ones, this change is accelerating the warming of the water and thereby accelerating climate change. The summer sea ice is predicted to almost completely disappear by 2030 as confirmed by the Intergovernmental Panel on Climate Change (IPCC), dooming animals like the polar bear and walrus to probable extinction. In 1990, I testified before Congress about the danger of the thawing permafrost which releases methane gas, a dangerous greenhouse gas, into the atmosphere. This process is now in motion. The record warm summers in the Arctic are advancing the thawing of the high elevations of the Greenland icecap. The loss of ice that we are now experiencing worldwide is the result of climate change.

Morally, we see very real impacts on the human race. The Inuit hunting culture depends on Arctic ice. The melting sea threatens to obliterate this culture, and also has repercussions that are felt around our world. With melting ice, low-lying island nations are being covered by rising sea waters. Intense hurricanes and other climate-related disruptions bankrupt our economies and threaten our societies.

I have never seen such drastic changes in the Arctic as quickly as I have in the last 15 years, and now these changes have become clear in my own Minnesota backyard. All Minnesotans are eyewitness to the warming winters and increasingly severe flood events. Scientists tell us we have ten years to make significant changes. With action, we can address the root causes and limit the impact.

How can we act to avert the worst consequences? Over the next ten years, we must significantly reduce our emissions. Action begins with education. Climate change must be an essential topic in the K-12 education curriculum. Because we are dealing with an immediate threat, we must mobilize and engage everyone. Congregations, environmental groups, youth organizations, campuses, clubs of all kinds play a pivotal role, informing and engaging their members and moving them towards action. We must expect that our leaders in government, industry, congregations, and schools are well informed about climate change and its consequences. Action also continues by decarbonizing our electric system and powering everything on renewable energy, as well as deploying conservation and energy efficiency.

This is the time we dig in. Climate change is a perfect challenge tailor-made for human ingenuity. I'm hopeful and confident we will rise to the challenge.

The climate impacts happening in the polar regions aren't confined geographically. Now we're all seeing the impacts; and seeing is believing.

We are all eyewitness to climate change.

And it's time we are all leaders in the movement to address it.

Will Steger

We Are All Witnesses

By Soni Shah and Kathleen Bacigalupi
Youth leaders taking climate action
First person account is by Soni Shah

"WHAT DO WE WANT?" Megaphone in hand, perched atop the steps, I shouted loudly as thousands of voices thundered back, "Climate Justice!" I felt empowered. My voice had been heard. People listened and responded to my plea. They, too, cherished our land along with the plants, animals and humans that live on it. This is about infinitely more than saving polar bears, I told them. Across the world humans are breathing in toxic chemicals or searching for shelter after catastrophic storms. It's extremely frustrating to see intense flooding outside my window coinciding with the rejection of multiple environmental bills, I yelled.

"WHEN DO WE WANT IT?" On September 20, 2019, as I marched with more than 8,000 fellow environmental activists from the Western Sculpture Garden to the Minnesota State Capitol Building, I had the privilege and honor to lead our chants. As I led, I experienced a deep sense of unity and a common desire for meaningful change: not only that we need it NOW, but that WE are capable of making this change happen. It gave me hope to watch thousands of students who share a loyalty to our Earth come together peacefully. I was given the courage to lead them; that day, I made a difference.

From the first moon landing to printing what has become the global currency, Americans pride themselves on being first. But when it comes to combating climate change, we are falling behind. We stay silent, viewing it as a distant problem.

Day after day, we continue to see the effects of our changing climate. The polar vortex last year brought Arctic cold to Minnesota, leaving homeless people scrambling for shelter. Each year at least 700 people who are homeless freeze to death in the U.S. This number will only increase as extreme temperatures continue to happen. We witness so-called "hundred-year floods" happening every five years, causing millions of dollars in damage. We experience more and more days over 90° F. We watch fires burning in California, Australia, and the Amazon. We witness the disrespect of Indigenous lands. We witness people in communities next to power plants, trash incinerators, and refineries breathing polluted air and suffering the health consequences—people who have contributed the least to causing the problems experiencing the worst impacts. Climate change is not just. We witness inaction and fighting in legislatures and Congress. We read the newest reports from scientists about the worsening of climate change, and understand we're running out of time.

Still, we are the climate generation. On the 50th anniversary of Earth Day, we stand united. We can continue to witness the destruction of our home, or we can witness the beginning of a new era. We can witness turning away, excuses, and fighting, or we can witness action. We can witness environmental justice. We can witness a green economy and a livable planet. We can witness the unity needed to solve the climate crisis. No matter who we are: black, white, or brown; they, he, or she; rich or poor; living in the city or the country; nine years old or ninety-nine, we are all witnesses.

Sonali Shah   Kathleen Bacigalupi

"I began to take notice of my senses... the feeling of crumbly, sun-warmed soil sifting through my toes, soft leaves brushing against my leg, the buzz of cicadas in the warm summer air, and the cool ribbons of shade created by the shadows of the corn stalks."

- Logan Reider, pg. 1

GRATITUDE

Losing A Refuge

As a young child in Minnesota, I enjoyed playing outside but didn't always feel the deep connection to the outdoors that many people experience in their very earliest memories.

For me it was a process of gradually becoming more attuned to the world around me and my place in it, as well as appreciating the vast opportunities and time for reflection that are abundant in nature.

I grew up in Delano, a small community in the western Twin Cities suburbs. Our home was situated on the edge of town, close to the woods and agricultural fields of rural Minnesota. My dad had always planted a large garden in our backyard, but I considered the garden chores tedious and I would seek to avoid them if possible.

As I grew older I began feeling more anxiety. I couldn't place the source, but as it mounted it began to cloud my thinking. Sometimes it was hard to see beyond the narrow scope of my worries.

One day my dad mentioned that the garden could use some weeding, and I thought focusing on a job would distract me from the inner tension I was feeling. As I began to work, the tension didn't disappear, but it shifted to the back of my mind. Slowly, it was replaced by an awareness of the moment, and I began to take notice of my senses... the feeling of crumbly, sun-warmed soil sifting through my toes, soft leaves brushing against my leg, the buzz of cicadas in the warm summer air, and the cool ribbons of shade created by the shadows of the corn stalks.

In a simple shift of perspective, I realized how spending so much time thinking about the unknowns of life had separated me from experiencing the peacefulness of the present moment.

In different areas of my life I had experienced self-doubt about my ability to contribute meaningful ideas and participate fully, and I realized that was part of why I felt anxious. I also became more aware of the many pressing issues in the world, like climate change. There was so much beyond my control, and I felt overwhelmed and powerless to make an impact.

The visible results of maintaining the garden helped me grow more confident in my ability to initiate a project and to handle challenges that came my way, allowing me to make a tangible difference through my own actions. Spending time in nature has allowed me to understand that I am just a small part of Earth's web of life, which can free me from feeling like I have to control things around me.

Last summer I had the opportunity to work on a local farm, and the impact of climate change in the garden and on the farm has been unmistakable.

A few years ago the large raspberry patch in my yard was invaded by nonnative species of fruit fly that is now able to survive the warmer winters in Minnesota, and the berry crop has been destroyed every year since. The heavier rains and warmer nighttime temperatures in the summer have allowed diseases like tomato blight to flourish and spread faster, creating huge losses in the harvests of many high-value crops throughout the entire state. At the same time that rainfall is increasing, a drought last summer parched the land for three weeks, and on the farm we needed to pull massive irrigation hoses through the rows of wilted plants just to keep them alive.

The destabilizing pattern of climate change has begun to upset the complex balances of the environment, gradually shifting it from being a refuge to escape anxiety, to becoming a source of anxiety for many people, myself included. It's disturbing to realize that many people throughout the world do not have this essential opportunity to reflect in nature because their surroundings have already been degraded by climate change and human activity.

I have often struggled with caring about issues but being unsure about concrete steps to take towards solutions. My ideas felt confined by a mindset that sees things as unchangeable, and I have begun to realize that this thinking is what enables difficult problems to keep occurring. Many people are deeply concerned about climate change, but they also don't know where to start. For me, our goal needs to be finding ways to make sustainable choices more accessible and help people expand their thinking to ask what changes really are possible.

Taking a first step is the hardest part for me and many others. I want other people to experience the same feeling of accomplishment and connection to the Earth that I do whenever I step into the garden, in whatever way fits their own life, and let themselves be inspired to take a step toward acting on climate change.

Logan Reider, Age 20
Delano, MN
Student / Caucasian / Concerned Youth

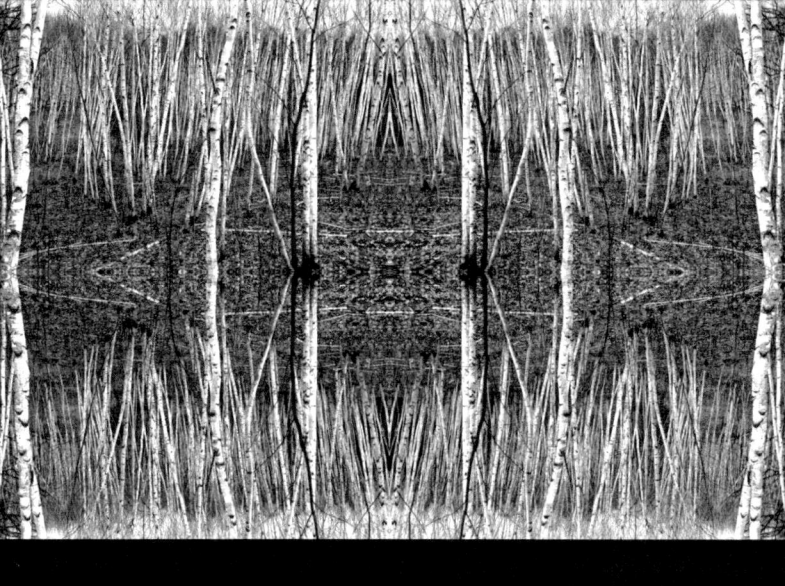

Birch Woods

My artwork is based on nature—its beauty, power, and meaning for us. For the most part my intent is to celebrate the natural world. "Birch Woods" is an example of that. To a large extent "nature art" is about what nature gives us aesthetically and spiritually. It is not about the fact that nature gives us life. That is taken for granted.

Basket

This piece is titled "BASKET" to mean "in abundance" and "acts of reciprocity." The purpose of showing a native prairie plant large and in detail, dried beyond recognition, is to draw attention to her beauty and the gifts she bestows at all stages of her life. She may appear dead, but her roots hold and sustain the soil's health; her stem is a refuge for hibernating insects; and her flower head provides seeds for birds who winter over.

I fear her gifts will be lost as the climate changes and makes our biomes shift in ways that leave us uncomfortable and uncertain. Listen to what she has to say about balance and reciprocity—pay attention to what native prairie plants need in order to thrive. Listen to Indigenous people; their wisdom and knowledge are essential to our survival. Bring back the buffalo as an act of reciprocity and the restoration of native prairie lands.

This artwork is inspired by participating in the Natural Heritage Project's unique exhibition "In Your Element." Artists were given a secret GPS setting and asked to spend time in their assigned "element," then return to the studio and create work based on their unique experience. I was assigned to Standing Cedars Land Conservancy near Osceola, WI. Where I stood was once farmland, now returned to dry prairie with a surprising list of native plants. That place is also known as Buffalo Skull.

Kristin Maija Peterson, Age 58
Saint Paul, MN
Visual Artist / Scandinavian / Beauty Hunter

EYEWITNESS | 6

The Cradle of Our Youth

I talked a lot as a kid.

If you know me, you might say that I still do. My mother told me that as a younger person, the only time I would stop talking was in the forest. She would strap me into a backpack kid-carrier, and we would walk through the woods behind our house.

My incessant and unintelligible babbling would cease the moment we passed under the massive red oaks that formed the gateway to a several-hundred-acre parcel that everyone in the neighborhood called "The Fire Trails." Named after the paths that criss-crossed the land to slow a forest fire, it was a magical strip of mature Laurentian hardwood forest that was set aside by the local paper mill along the banks of the St. Louis River. It hadn't been logged since the virgin pine stands were cleared from the land and floated downriver.

It wasn't unusual to come across giant white pine stumps left by the flames of the 1918 fire and preserved under the maple, aspen, and oak canopy. I spent most of my free time while growing up exploring this piece of nature that, to me, seemed endless in its capacity to captivate me and calm me through the unsavory experience of being an awkward teenager.

The best cure I've ever found for a broken heart is to lie down on the forest floor and listen to the wind and watch the trees sway.

I saw this healing power of nature at work time after time as a guide in the Northern Minnesota border country; each camper would come out of the wilderness different from when they entered. I've been thinking a lot lately about nature's power to calm and give a much-needed perspective on things. I can't think of anything this world needs more of now than a deep breath and some time to listen.

I'm sharing my personal relationship with the natural world because I believe we need to examine that personal connection if we are to be effective ambassadors for the planet.

I have been teaching environmental literacy to young people for over fifteen years, and no matter how charming I am, no human teacher can compare to the relationship a person forms with the natural world.

Mother Nature is her own best advocate.

We are faced with an environmental crisis that has the potential to alter our natural world in profound ways. Warnings of sea level rise, mosquito-borne illnesses, and summer heat waves have done little to sway public opinion.

I talk with young people frequently about climate change, and they are well aware of the danger of continuing on our current path. The message they are getting is that "if we don't do something about climate change things are going to get very bad." I don't want youth to be motivated only by the fear of what is to come.

I think we might have better luck if we are all motivated by the love of what is here now.

I would like to leave you with this request. Go out and listen to the natural world and bring a friend. Mother Nature is an amazing communicator. She can make anyone fall in love with her if they take the chance to let her whisper in their ear.

Danny Friedman, Age 40
Duluth, MN
Artist / Jewish / Lover of Shenanigans

Superior Sunrise

The Great Lakes contain 21% of the world's fresh water. Climate change is already impacting our lakes in many ways: increasing temperatures, increasing levels of bacteria, and increasing presence of invasive species. "Superior Sunrise" represents the potential opportunity to save our precious natural resources like Lake Superior by taking action. Every change made today to curb the rate of climate change can build into waves of positive impact that will ensure the sustainability of the Great Lakes for generations to come.

Kat Nottingham, Age 56
Eagan, MN
Artist / Caucasian / Water Conservation Enthusiast

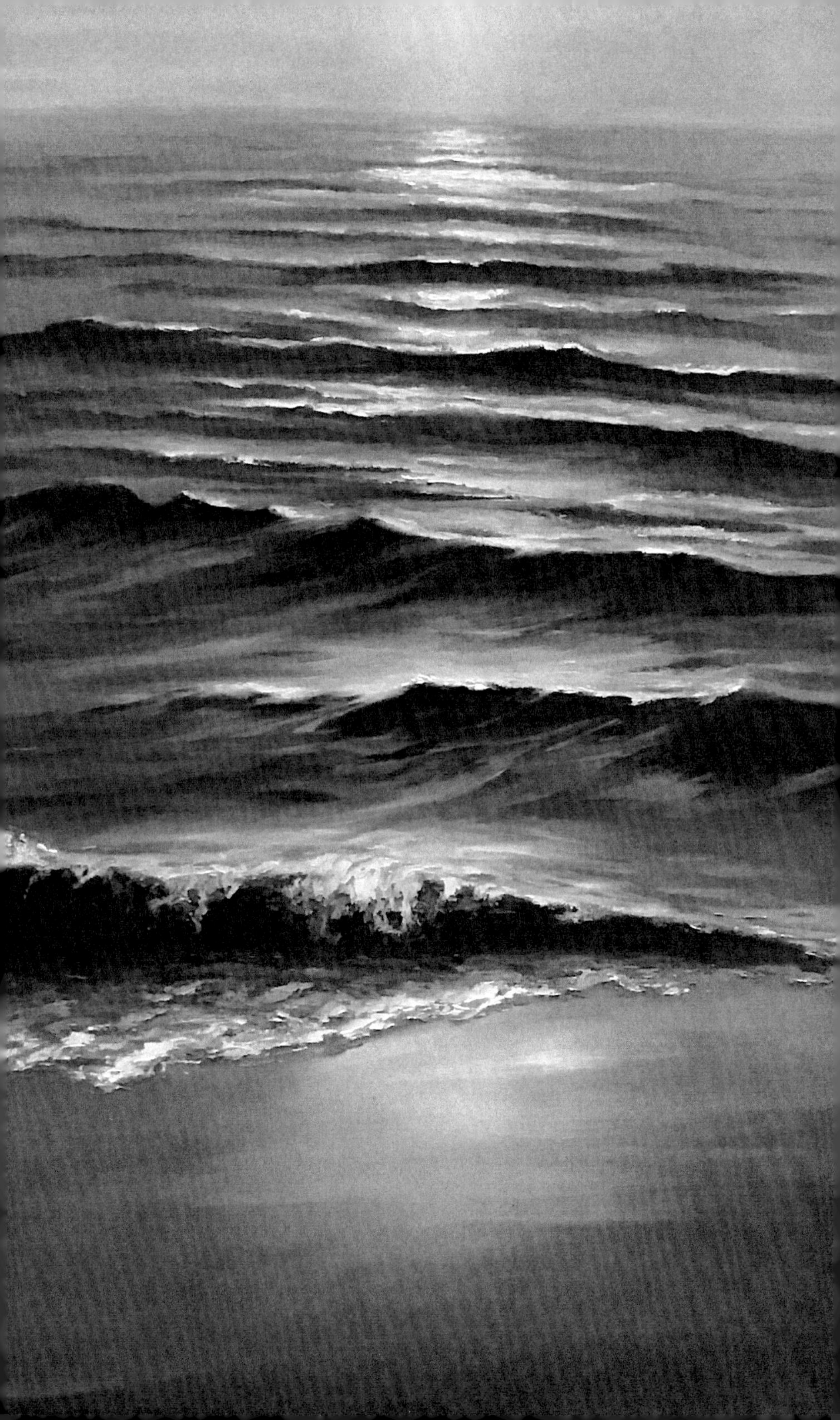

Author's note: *More often than not, we are presented with facts and figures about climate change. As a climate scientist, I have firsthand experience of this effort to connect with the minds of people through logical thinking. My poem takes a different approach, drawing the reader's attention to the heart through their sensory experience of climate change. Each stanza begins with a question referring to one of the five senses. Each question is followed by a symbolic reference from nature, e.g. a whippoorwill sounding a call of warning or a storm made stronger by human-induced greenhouse gas emissions. Two stanzas include words from local Indigenous language: Mni (Dakota for water) and Manoomin (Ojibwe for wild rice). The poem concludes with a final question inviting the reader into partnership. I believe that partnership with each other is the best and perhaps the only way to transcend vicious cycles of blame, pain, and shame.*

Do You Sense It?

Did you hear that?
The whip-poor-will,
hidden in your heart,
singing a song of warning.

Did you smell that?
The south wind,
your exhalation,
fueling stronger storms.

Did you see that?
Glimmer of light
shining silently
on the horizon.

Did you taste that?
Mni, life-giving water,
moving through you now
like a watershed.

Did you touch that?
Manoomin, wild rice,
bowing with gratitude
as it grows on the water.

And do you sense the new way
inviting us again
into the joyful murmur
of partnership?

```
Brian Smoliak, Age 35
Minneapolis, MN
Climate Entrepreneur / White / Night Gardener
```

On the Edge of Something Wild

I explore wonder and mindfulness through photographing nature's presence in urban-bound landscapes and representing this presence through abstracted, micro imagery. As the climate changes, our experience and relationship with nature become abstracted and distant. It takes more effort to feel connected to the Earth, to climate and to the power of nature. I feel this strain especially in urban environments where nature is shaped and tamed to fit into the landscape. My hope is for this imagery to represent nature as a mystical, powerful force lurking in our urban landscape.

Kait Macheledt, Age 27
Minneapolis, MN
STEMM Researcher / Woman / Intersectional Feminist

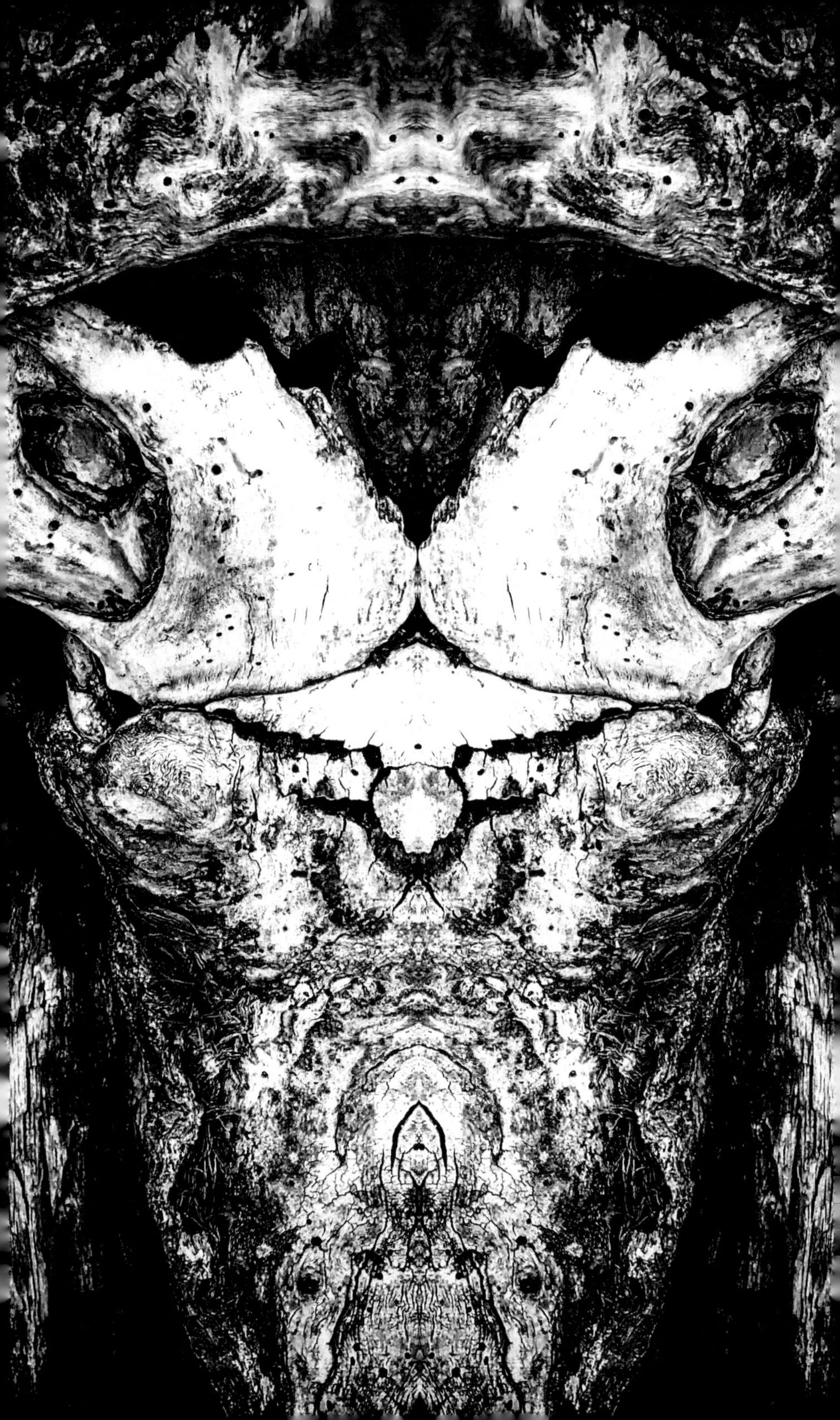

"Listen to their stories pouring like shattered glass through the other side of the wall."

- DansAlux, pg.17

LOSS

Los Caminantes

Los Caminantes se acercan
Can't you hear their pain?
Their fields cracked
under a burning air
breathed out by
the Great North Boss.

Listen to their stories
pouring like shattered glass
through the other side of the wall.
It won't cut you:
pick up the little pieces
with which your freedom was built,
assemble a bridge
or sprinkle them on the soil
and watch what grows.

On the deadly dry path
—with the resilience built
after Mitch and
after the bloodshed of the poor—
los Caminantes vienen
con el pecho abierto
donde colocan los hijos
que les quedan.

The walkers/travelers come near

*The travelers come
With their chests open
Where they keep the children
That are left to them/remain.*

```
DansAlux, Age 42
Minneapolis, MN
Performer / Honduran / Educator
```

The Work

Climate change sits in my gut like stones
in the pockets of my clothes
pulling me under water
after I have jumped in.

I must deliberately work to remove each stone, examine it, determine
its weight.

Climate change is like a shadow
constantly following me—
sometimes revealed by a burst of sun—
lengthening and growing as time moves forward.

Climate change sits on my shoulders
as a burden to carry.
I feel the burden lighten
with good people,
in green spaces,
hearing the crunch of snow beneath my feet,
with the touch of my children,
the embrace of my spouse,
with the marching of many feet, and
through the voices of passionate leaders.

```
Kristen Iverson Poppleton, Age 45
Saint Paul, MN
Climate Change Professional / Winter Enthusiast / Mother
```

For the Love of Winter

I'm a desert girl who wants to save our iconic Minnesota winter.

I grew up in Arizona falling in love with the desert, bright yellow and orange flowers that thrive in seemingly barren land, the warm breezes that carry the smell of the Palo Verde trees, learning "desert survival" like what to do if a gila monster bites you, not to trust your sister when she says to touch a cactus, hiking mountains, and sitting on red rocks gazing over valleys that stretch for as far as you can see while small lizards scurry in the hot sun next to you.

But, I also fell in love with Minnesota. I grew up spending my summers in Minnesota at my family's cottage on beautiful, clean Pelican Lake, about four hours north of Minneapolis. So, with winters in Arizona and summers in Minnesota, I never really experienced a cold winter except for an occasional trip to ski or a family outing up north to play in the snow for a weekend hike.

I found winter my first year in college in Flagstaff, Arizona, where it does get cold enough to snow. However, it wasn't until I attended the University of Minnesota in Duluth that I fell in love with winter. I chose Minnesota to start my family. What a great place for my son to grow up. Igloos, forts, cross-country skiing, sledding, hot chocolate, mittens, fires, snowy Christmases... and survival. We are survivors. My family in Arizona would call in amazement to find out how we were surviving the sub-zero weather.

My son joined the cross-country ski team in high school. The first year was fun. They practiced in nearby woods. But, then it happened. We had a couple of winters with hardly any snow. The cross-country ski team became more like a cross-country track team. They ran instead of skiing. They had snow hauled in a truck and dumped on a field. They shoveled snow to have a small track to practice. Meets were cancelled. It was devastating to me, but not just because of the problems with cross-country skiing. I was filled with fear. Is this what winters would now become? Brown and muddy everywhere, and not white and pristine, crisp and clean?

But, while I was sad, others were happy. What a beautiful, mild winter we were having. People laughed at the water skier skiing on a lake at a time of the year when the lake should've been frozen. The water skier's picture made the paper. How great this is! I felt alone and sad, not understanding why people could think a winter like this was wonderful.

When I questioned and voiced my concern, I felt like I was being ridiculed for not being able to just enjoy the mild temperatures. I was being overreactive. I was told to relax, this is just cyclical. I knew differently.

But I didn't know what to do.

I began to talk with people who also cared about climate change, and I realized I wasn't alone. I'm a film producer, and now I'm using my video skills to share inspiring stories of people, businesses and organizations working to tackle the climate crisis. My hope through sharing stories is to teach, inspire, and empower people to do things differently for the planet.

My love of winter remains, and I hope that sharing stories will bring the message of saving winters to my home state of Minnesota.

I don't feel so alone anymore. I feel hope, and I'm excited for more people to start sharing their stories to influence positive change.

```
Erika Gilsdorf, Age 52
Detroit Lakes, MN
Video Producer / Mother
Earth Lover
```

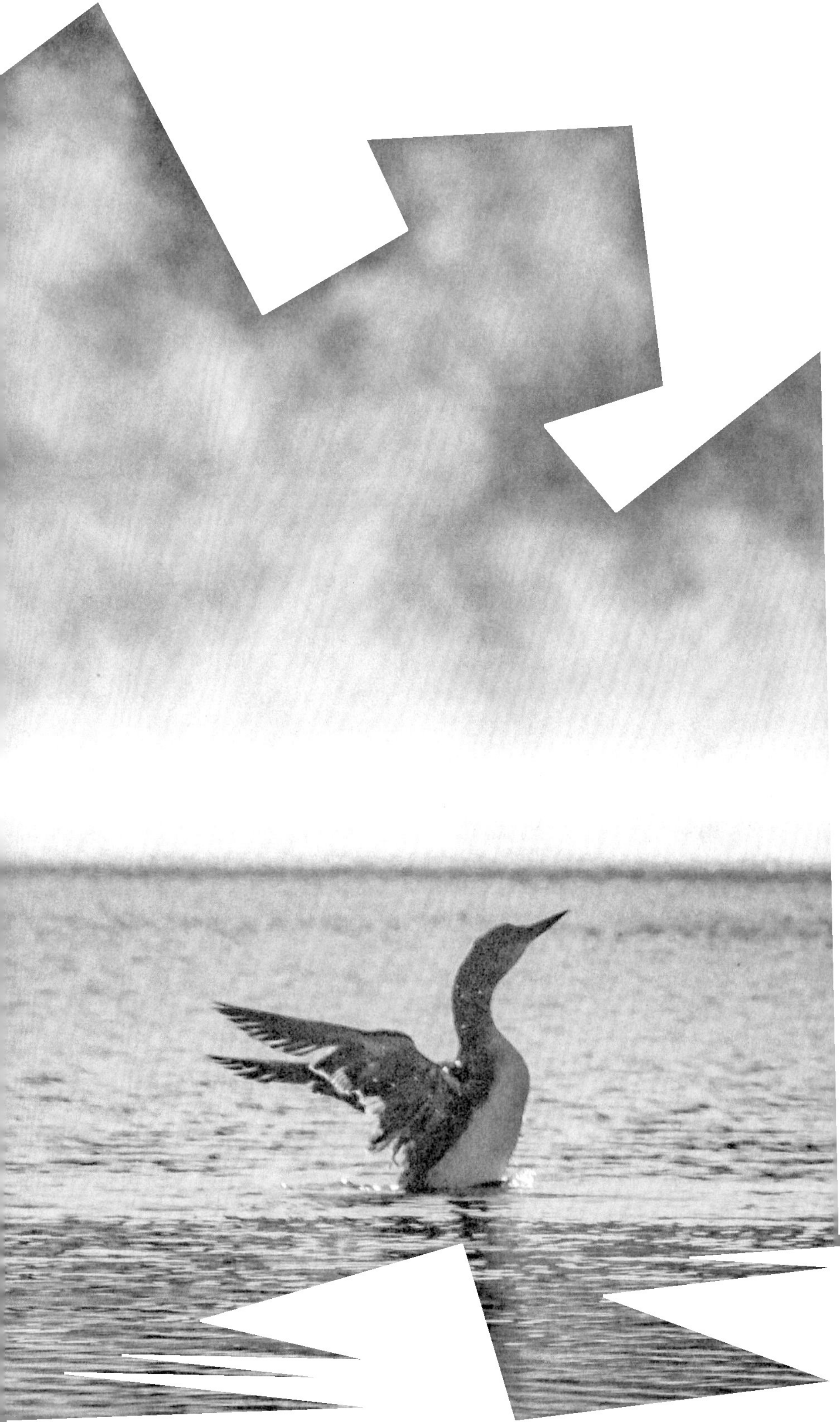

The Loons Soon May Be Leaving; Minnesota Will Be Grieving

Loons. Everyone who has seen them on a lake and heard their long, haunting wails adores them. No wonder they are our State Bird. With red eyes, black head, white breast, black and white striped neck, and speckled back, they are the essence of the lake country. They inspire our love and nostalgia, thousands of photos, the naming of athletic teams, and endless paraphernalia.

And now I'm told that loons will disappear from Minnesota because of climate change.

Loons were in our lakes before the pyramids were built 3,000 years ago. Even before humans first lived here 6,000 years ago, the loons followed the retreating glaciers. An ancient species, closest North American relative of penguins, their ancestors date back more than a hundred million years.

My parents and we four brothers first came to our lake in the late 1950s to outfit and guide wilderness canoe trips. Now, our extended family shares vacations at the family compound; it's the glue that holds our far-flung gang together. We have always had a nesting pair of loons on our small lake. We follow them closely each year, reporting to each other about the progress of the chicks, when they have disappeared for a day, sharing our fears that an eagle or turtle has eaten them, and our heartfelt relief when they reappear.

And now I learn that this quintessential symbol of the north woods won't be here when the newest child in our extended family, born on my 80th birthday, is old enough to be a grandmother.

It doesn't have to be that way. If we can limit global temperature increase to 1.5 degrees C, loon habitat will be diminished but not destroyed, at least in the northern half of the state.

Heading into my ninth decade, my fervent hope is that by the time I have taken my last portage, we will have figured this climate problem out, and that the almost vertical curve of CO_2 increase since the 1950s will level out and head downwards.

We know we can address climate change. We already have the tools. We just need the political will.

Charles K. Dayton, Age 80
Ely, MN
Climate Activist / Retired Environmental Lawyer / Grandparent

National Parks

I want to visit all the national parks someday.
Because with everything that's going on,
in the environment,
in the world,
I worry that those national parks,
like beautiful Voyageurs
on Minnesota's northern border,
won't be there anymore,
or they won't be the same.
I want to visit all the national parks,
but I want to leave behind no trace,
I want the national parks to easily forget
that I was ever there.
I want children someday
and I want them to walk the same trails,
following in my footsteps.
I want them to know what it feels like
to feel so free
in a world that can make you feel
like you're always behind
and falling apart.
I want them to smell trees and hear birds,
I want them to breathe,
like really breathe,
air that's not filled with poisons.
I want to visit all the national parks,
I want to heal the earth,
I want better for
this world of ours.

```
Marie Osuna, Age 20
Forest Lake, MN
Student / Mixed Race / Volunteer
```

Ascension

When at last
it tilted worse to land than leave
what happened was this: the birds
snipped their gravitational strands.

They took two or three or five final
wing strokes heavenward
and on that momentum traveled,
up and out.

Kingdom, Phylum,
Class: Aves
The birds folded their
splendor, resisted
iridescence, overrode
any hint of song.
They closed their eyes above the cumulus,
did not look back,
froze solid in rising,
and rose still,
a funeral flood of billions.

Lamented as they passed
by sundog, aurora, diamond dust,
lauded by thunder,
they sailed into darkness
beyond atmosphere's reach,
then drifted out,
a debris field in the silence of space,
a marker.

It was not predicted.
All were bent upon
the other forms of mass extinction.

But now
in retrospect,
in the catastrophic mourning,
it can be understood.
This was earth's
death leavening,
with all that followed here
merely
decomposition.

Author's note: *I am a birder. This is a hobby that gives me, and many others like me, a great deal of pleasure. Like many other birders, I participate in a citizen science project through Cornell Lab of Ornithology which requires us to count and submit lists of every bird we are able to identify during any given outing. This data, collected from thousands of birders all over the world, is crucial to learning the story of bird breeding, migration patterns, and population. In September of 2019, we heard the news that North America's bird population has dropped by three billion since 1970. Climate change is a key factor in this process (habitat shift, habitat loss, inundation of coastal areas, increasingly severe weather, etc.). When I am out birding, and keeping my counts, I sometimes feel that I am documenting the extinction of these incredible animals. My poem reflects on this dynamic.*

Janet Malotky, Age 62
Shorewood, MN
Speech-language Pathologist / Caucasion / Birder

A Future Memory of Cold
_____

My two youngest children enjoyed playing on Eagle Lake, near our home in Maple Grove, Minnesota. I remember wondering as I watched them if their children (or grandchildren) will know what it is like to walk out on a frozen lake.

James Matthew Pipkin, Age 48
Maple Grove, MN
Aerospace Engineer / Minnesotan / Concerned Father

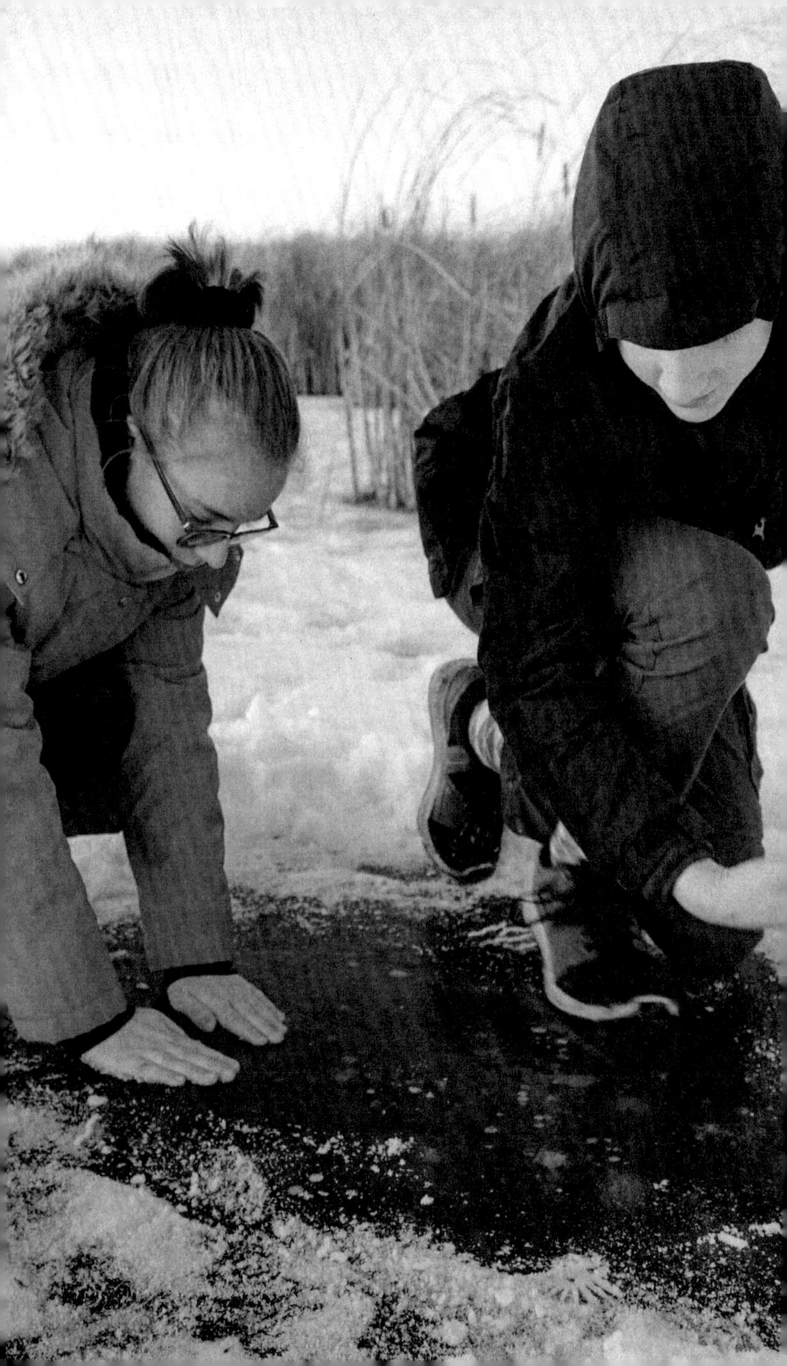

Everything Is Connected

Some of my most fond memories growing up on a farm were of baling hay. Picking up hay bales involved mostly play for my five siblings and me: rolling the bales to an ideal position for lifting, making forts in them on the hay wagon, or sliding along the grass behind the wagon. These memories are precious to me, because they are filled with family and neighbors.

Now, as an adult, I am still baling hay, and I know first-hand the real work that is required. Somehow, amidst the hard physical labor, the sweetness of baling is still so real: the smell of hay, and the... all of the happiness and fullness I have felt in years past comes back. I am so grateful to be farming on this Dakota land where I was raised and which I feel connected to.

I farm in Franconia Township on the land where I grew up. My parents have always had a diversified hobby farm, and four years ago I took on running the vegetable CSA (Community Supported Agriculture) farm that my mom started 10 years ago; Shepherd Moon Farm. We maintain the health of the soil through crop rotation, limited tilling, cover crops, mulching, and using compost to replenish nutrients. This makes for vigorous crops, soil that is rich and alive, and clean water. I farm because I love being on the land and I want to provide food for my community and support a healthy rural economy.

But the truth is, the farm economy is not working for farmers, and it is not working for the Earth. Our current agricultural system devalues people, degrades the soil and water, and contributes enormously to climate change. Farmers are in debt. The majority of us need an off-farm income to get by.

And the climate crisis is making this worse. As increased rains flood our Midwest fields, more farmers are forced to depend on government-funded crop insurance. We would much rather be funded to lead solutions and feed people.

Minnesota's climate has grown wetter and warmer, which means in addition to flooded fields we have new pests and diseases that were never an issue when I was a kid. Spotted wing drosophila now devours our berries. Our wet seasons spread black rot more rapidly, killing cabbage, broccoli, and other brassicas.

This year, tomato harvests were terrible for many farmers and home-growers I talked to, due to rain-carried diseases. Almost every tomato I harvested from the field was diseased, and I got a tenth of my usual yield. The rest was too damaged by the time it ripened, and it went to the animals. If I had not put in a hoop house the year before (where I control the water conditions as California growers do with irrigation) and grown another crop of tomatoes there, I would not have been able to provide any tomatoes to customers.

Minnesota is not alone in its challenges. California growers produce more than half of all vegetables for the US. But climate change has accelerated their water crisis, and they are draining the last drops from their aquifers. If we want to keep feeding each other, it is time to rise to the challenge.

We farmers know that we need to lead, so we are talking to each other. This winter I met with 30 vegetable growers from the region to share strategies for coping with the climate crisis. There was an incredible amount of experience in that room. We talked vegetable varieties, tillage, nutrient management, and more. I learned of a broccoli fungus that has been creeping northward with the warming climate, so I can expect it this year.

We are supporting each other, but we also need institutional support. Conventional corn and soybean rotation inhibits the living things in the soil and leaves the land bare for most of the year. The University of Minnesota created this system with the goal of higher yields, but those yields come at a cost to the soil, water, our health, and the climate.

Our land grant university should be supported in creating an alternative way, an agriculture system that is economically viable for farmers, with continuous living cover that builds soil health, captures carbon, and is good for ecosystems and people.

Like the warm memories I have of putting up hay with my neighbors as a kid, the future I see depends on our community. I imagine us neighbors working together: rotating animals on each others' lands, under solar panels that power our homes, sharing equipment, and trading ideas with each other to face new challenges.

This is what gives me hope. We are some of the communities being hit the hardest by climate change in Minnesota. And we are thinking, and determined to be part of the solution.

Julie Arnold, Age 29
Lindstrom, MN
Farmer / White / Vegetable Lover

Adieu

I mean not to bid my home farewell
but will it remain after I have gone?
Will I return not to emerald pathways and
clandestine waters,
but to a wasteland,
a cemetery of dreams?
Oh, Minnesota,
will you hold on for me when I am no longer
young?
Will I ever dance in your fields
once your memory fades?
Let this kiss be not a goodbye.

Author's note: "Adieu" focuses on my hope that beautiful Minnesota can survive climate change so that I can return to it. I hope our state thrives so that Minnesotans of the future may experience its wonders rather than only reading about them in history books.

```
Rosella Joyce, Age 15
Albertville, MN
Quirky / Book-addicted / Feminist
```

Climate Change in Northern Minnesota: Spruce, Maple or Savanna?

To a forest ecologist, Minnesota is one of the most interesting places on the planet, where three biomes come together: boreal forest (spruce, fir, pine and birch), temperate deciduous forest (oak, maple and basswood), and savanna, grasslands with scattered trees. That's why I moved here 31 years ago—I arrived in 1988 as a post-doc in Margaret Davis' world-renowned paleoecology lab at the University of Minnesota. We used fossil pollen in bog sediments to study how forests responded to episodes of climate change thousands of years ago.

Shortly after I arrived, the first big public discussion of climate change occurred as a result of the extremely hot and droughty summer of 1988. NASA scientist James Hansen testified before Congress that hot summers, along with sea level rise and other important impacts of a warming climate, could become commonplace in the future.

Such a change in climate could potentially have much larger impacts on Minnesota's forests than the massive amount of logging that occurred at the time of European settlement from the mid-1800s to the early 1900s. After that cutover, even though it took down most of the saleable timber, the ecological rules for recovery of the forest ecosystems were still the same as during the last few thousand years, and the young post-logging forests started their recovery back towards historic conditions.

With a warming climate, however, everything is different in the 21st century, and the location and character of Minnesota's three biomes could change dramatically. We could even lose the boreal biome that contains one-third of our state's biodiversity.

The magnitude of change in Minnesota will depend on CO2 emissions over the next several decades. Looking at the evidence of forest change in response to past periods of climate change, in 1988 I supposed that if the state continued in the "business as usual" scenario for burning fossil fuels, the forests in northern Minnesota would likely be replaced by grasslands. Evidence that has come out since 1988 supports that supposition. If anything, scientists in 1988 were conservative in their estimates of the magnitude of warming, with actual warming so far being greater than predicted at the time.

During the 30-plus years since 1988, I have worked with a number of talented graduate students and faculty colleagues at the University of Minnesota to carry out the science needed to reveal how forests respond to warming climate. Why did the grassland-forest border encountered by European settlers cross Minnesota from northwest to southeast? What prevents maple and oak species from successfully colonizing boreal forests in northeastern Minnesota?

We discovered that the balance between boreal and temperate forest is primarily determined by summer temperature, with boreal forests clinging to places in northeastern Minnesota where mean summer temperatures are less than 65 degrees, putting oak and maple at a competitive disadvantage. Annual water balance determines the interactions between forests and grasslands. The historic northwest to southeast grassland-forest border across Minnesota sat right where this balance was zero; northern and eastern Minnesota had positive water balances and were forested while southern and western Minnesota had negative water balances and had landscapes of grasslands/savannas.

These results led to two more questions: where will we find places with summers cool enough to support boreal forest, and places moist enough to support forests of any sort, in a much warmer climate? Our most recent research results as of 2019 show that for a business-as-usual CO_2 emissions scenario, the grassland-forest border would push 200 miles to the northeast, and northern Minnesota would be warm enough for temperate tree species like oak and maple.

By 2070, most of the state would support vast expanses of grasslands and savannas, with maple and oak forests in the tip of the Arrowhead—in other words, Minnesota would be the "New Kansas." On the other hand a reduced CO_2 emissions scenario—80% reduction by 2050—

would result in a barely detectable shift in biome boundaries, and the Minnesota that we recognize today would still be here.

By the end of the 21st century, will we become the "New Kansas," or a slightly modified version of the existing Minnesota? We could easily achieve the latter with a quick transition to renewable energy, tree-planting and regenerative agriculture. The choice between these two alternative scenarios depends on society at large. In Minnesota we can only make a minor contribution to the needed reduction in fossil fuel use. The rest of the world needs to cooperate—if not, then Minnesotans will be passive passengers on a ride to Kansas.

However, there is one thing I am sure of. Although boreal forests don't care whether or not they grow in Minnesota, people do care. Perhaps the desire to maintain a sense of place in Minnesota and throughout the world will spur people to take action to reduce CO_2 emissions.

```
Lee Frelich, Age 62
Minneapolis, MN
Scientist / White / Tree Expert
```

Change

My parents' home is about 10 feet from a lake. As temperatures rise and there is less snow to keep the ice on the lake down, it pushes further into their coastline, causing irreparable damage. Over time they will lose more and more of their property until eventually, their house itself will be in jeopardy. My artwork depicts this violent process with a figure representing the ice as an ephemeral and jagged force moving towards the coastline. It takes up only part of the image though, because its effects can be remedied by intentional and immediate action on the part of our leaders.

Kyle Leonard Bernier, Age 26
Roseville, MN
Art Therapist and Counselor / Caucasian
Environmentally-Conscious Printmaker

A Hunter's View

Every generation of hunters has heard of the previous one's "good old days." But rarely does one generation see the good old days come and go.

Few people are as attuned to the weather as hunters. It dictates much of their activity, since it dictates much of their prey's activity. And while weather and climate are not one and the same, the changing climate has indeed produced weather that has impacted hunting.

Query Minnesota's hunters and you'll hear many laments about how things have changed, and not for the better.

One of the most glaring examples is how our longer, warmer autumns have affected duck hunting. Once our locally raised ducks are wised up, duck hunters wait for the northern ducks to arrive on their way south. Historically, ducks filtered into Minnesota with each cold front. Some pulses were so predictable you could schedule vacation time for hunting and be pretty confident that "new" ducks would be here. For me, it was the third week of October, and for four decades I would set that week aside to spend in the marsh. Sure, there were slow years when the weather didn't cooperate, but they were rare.

Not any longer. Warm weather persists now well into November, and not just in Minnesota, but into Canada. With no cold fronts to stimulate migration, ducks are content to stay to the north. Where once the cold air descended like a slow curtain, freezing the Canadian provinces before it reached Minnesota, in recent decades, the curtain falls all at once, and that hard, quick freeze pushes ducks quickly through our state. It has even caused them to make complete "flyovers" with no stops in Minnesota.

For those who love the marsh and its magic, who love the days with friends and family in a duck blind, these changes have been more than disappointing. They bring profound sadness.

There have been other changes as well. Those of you who are deer hunters probably remember when tracking in snow during most of the firearms deer season was normal. Today that is increasingly rare.

Too hot to run your hunting dog in Minnesota? Who'd have thought that could be possible? It rarely was, before. Now, when grouse or pheasant hunting, there are an increasing number of days when dogs must be watched closely for heat exhaustion.

Remember moose hunting? I was one of the lucky ones to draw a permit three decades ago. Now there is no longer a moose season here. While climate change is not the sole cause of Minnesota's declining moose numbers, every biologist agrees that the added stress caused by hotter summers, and the proliferation of winter ticks due to earlier springs, are serious contributing factors to the decline of this iconic Minnesota species.

Some will say that we should just get used to these changes.

That's a future we shouldn't accept. We are a state rich with hunting legacy, one that defines many of us. We must act now to preserve what we can of that heritage.

Michael Furtman, Age 65
Duluth, MN
Hunter / Nature Writer
Photographer

EYEWITNESS | 38

"Our state has people who are rich in spirit, and a culture that is all about sharing our gifts and talents with a deep generosity. This is a "seize the day" opportunity for us."

- Mark Seeley, pg.43

RESPONSIBILITY

Seize the Day

Building on an obsessive interest in weather that started when my wife and I were VISTA volunteers in Utah, I earned a PhD in climate science in the 1970s and was hired for a newly created faculty position as a Climate Science Educator with the University of Minnesota Extension Service. Human-caused climate change was not talked about in the 1970s.

I knew that Minnesota was a people place, a place to raise my family and to enjoy the rich natural resources that are here. It was the opportunity I was looking for, working with people. I spent the rest of my career, from 1978 to 2018, helping to maintain the state Climate's Database and educating the public, translating what the data meant for our lives and livelihoods in Minnesota.

Though I did not grow up in Minnesota, my roots are here. It is the place where my great-great-grandfather Ira Seeley started his family, and where my grandfather sowed seeds in the rich soil. What I would later come to know intimately is that Minnesota is also a paradise for those who work in weather and climate. In Minnesota we get to experience every sort of weather variation and climate element that you can imagine. It was in Minnesota that I found my place both personally and professionally.

A turning point for me on climate change happened in 1988, when NASA scientist James Hansen testified at a US Congressional hearing, where he declared "with 99% confidence that a recent sharp rise in temperatures was a result of human activity." I spoke out against his statement in an article for the *Star Tribune,* saying that we should look at natural climate cycles before concluding that humans are influencing our climate.

However, in the 1990s the data itself woke me up to the reality that Minnesota's climate was dramatically changing. What I observed through our state's climate network and the records being set was alarming and overwhelming. As a caretaker and user of the state database, I noticed that we were recording unprecedented temperature patterns, heat index values, rainfall events, flash floods, and dew points. The behavior of the data was impossible to ignore and made me realize we were not prepared to deal with all of the consequences of climate change already underway in our state. I knew that I had a responsibility to tell people what I was seeing.

Since then climate change has become even more manifest. When you are a scientist, you have to pay attention to what the data are telling you, and when it is compelling you have to act. The decade of the 1990s in Minnesota was our wettest in history. This "climate fact" transformed the thinking of a lot of climate scientists (including myself). Further, it was becoming clear that these changes were indeed primarily induced by human factors, mainly landscape change and greenhouse gas emissions.

In the late 1990s to early 2000s, climate change became contentious, not only on the floor of the US Congress but in our own Minnesota Legislature. I was called to legislative hearings to talk about our climate history and to share the recent data. I shared that something distinct was happening here, and it was not just natural cycles.

After translating this truth in the most pragmatic way, I became frustrated by those who refused to accept the science. Since then I have made a commitment to educate people about climate change, the whole truth of it, and how it has and will have consequences on nearly everything that we care about. In 2006, I wrote *The Minnesota Weather Almanac,* the first comprehensive book on our state's climate history. I quickly learned that the data were changing so rapidly that an updated version of the book would be needed. In 2015, I released the second edition, pointing out that in less than 10 years more than 17,000 daily climate records had been broken in the state observing network, and 165 new state records had been established, mostly for daily temperature and precipitation. This unprecedented pace of climate change is analogous to the level of change that used to be measured over thousands of years.

Climate change is a huge challenge for us to cope with. I am not afraid to speak candidly of the urgency for us all to respond. Minnesota should be leading in solutions to climate change. The longer we delay action and allow lawmakers not to recognize the urgency of the problem, the worse it will be for future generations.

I am proud to say that Minnesota's history has shown many admirable political leaders who have applied knowledge in pragmatic ways that benefit all of our residents, not just the rich few. Our lawmakers today need to find ways to incentivize strategies and solutions that will help us adapt to climate change that is already occurring and mitigate the pace of change for the future. Not doing so will put management of our natural resources and our societal infrastructure at great risk.

In Minnesota we are blessed to have diverse and rich natural resources, and we should all be concerned about preserving what makes this home so special. Our state has people who are rich in spirit and a culture that is all about sharing our gifts and talents with a deep generosity.

This is a "seize the day" opportunity for us.

Mark W. Seeley, Age 72
Saint Paul, MN
Scientist / Educator / Concerned Citizen

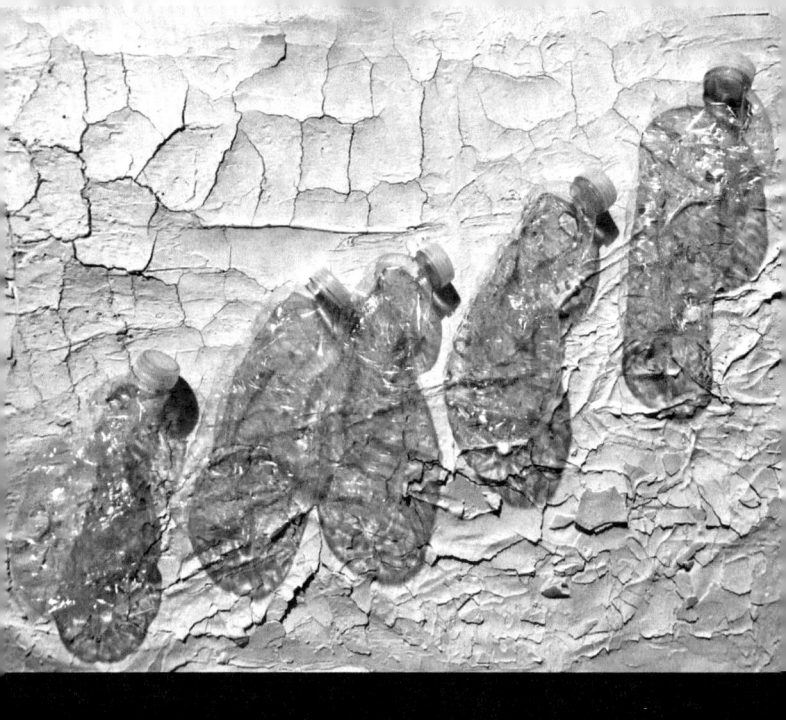

The Penitents

My work portrays the aftermath of our disregard for the climate problem. It shows a line of penitent people (represented here as empty and indistinct wrinkled plastic water bottles) climbing to an uncertain place through the dry landscape they have generated.

Javier Elias Carrasco Miock, Age 52
Maple Grove, MN
Visual Artist / Musician Composer

Misiziibi—Great River
___

Fur traders
    &
        slave raiders
           &
                Industrial coal-agers
They
    Claimed Her
        as
            their savior
                yet
They
    Miss
      iss
        ippi
            Treated Her
                    F
                    O
                    U
                    L
    MESS
      iss
          ippi
        pollutants what
They
                          Gave Her
        as
They
        harassed,
        molested,
            and then
                              Raped Her

                        that's how
They
        Repaid Her
                    in return
                    for all
                                    Her
                    favors
                        &
                        Now
We
            Piddle,
            Peddle,
            Paddle,
                    fast
                past   our
                    dirty
                    ugly
        PAST
            in a desperate attempt
                            to try
                            &
                            Save
Ourselves
            from
                self-destruction
                            in the
            form of
EXPLODING......Green House Gas

Michael Chaney, Age 67
Minneapolis, MN
Ag Patriot / African American / Thought Leader

The Currency of War

My grandfather, Wolde Tensae, passed away when I was 19 years old, only five years after I met him. He was an Eritrean citizen from the region of Keren. Eritrea is a country located in the horn of Africa just north of Ethiopia and Somalia. It was one of the few colonies of Italy and officially became a country in 1997.

Just a year later Eritrea was at war, a conflict that began as a minor border dispute and escalated. The ethnic clashes and other political differences that ensued are too complicated and painful to include. The war unofficially lasted until June 2000, resulting in the deaths of hundreds of thousands of people from both Ethiopia and Eritrea.

The implications of war are many, and during those years severe drought resulted in famine, particularly because most government funds were being spent on weapons and other war instrumentation. My grandfather used to say that living in between Ethiopia and Eritrea was one of the most difficult things for him, as he witnessed the famine, major sanitation problems, and stripping of the land, and saw the death of many people on a daily basis.

I am still not sure how my environmental ethics fit within the climate crisis and the way I feel cherished by the Earth, but I do know that there are many things war takes away from us. The loss of connection to the land, and of so many cherished lives, is the currency of war. I don't know what my grandpa would say if he were alive today, but he wouldn't try to connect the crisis of the climate we are facing today to warfare. But I can see that warfare is a symptom of climate change. Even here in the United States, our military has said that climate change is a threat multiplier that exacerbates conflict.

My relationship with the natural world was always transactional until I moved to a place called Minnesota where water and other natural beings were abundant around me. I saw no famine, no sanitation problems and no shortage of firewood. Amid this abundance, I was able to see the privilege I have come to possess, a privilege so great it has left me with a responsibility of trying to inspire other people's kinship with the Earth.

My privilege was left to me by my grandfather, who experienced the loss of this connection. It has driven my passion to dedicate my life to joining with others to address the injustices that we are causing to the Earth, and therefore to those who are unable to speak for themselves.

War is a symptom of a changing climate, and it is an incomplete story. I am not here to finish the story my grandfather started, but I am here to add to it. I hope I get to fulfill that part of my duty in the most genuine and human way possible.

```
Yordanose Solomone, Age 24
Minneapolis, MN
Daughter / Immigrant / Activist
```

Aboard the Pequod

Whale dies in Thailand after eating more than 80 plastic bags
—Fox News headline, June 4, 2018

Today at Costco I bought
a 30 pack of Charmin wrapped in plastic.
Inside the plastic bag
were three more plastic bags,
each containing 10 rolls.

I also ate a tiny sample of acai sorbet,
topped with fresh organic strawberries and blueberries
and a sprinkling of organic quinoa.
It was served in a tiny plastic bowl
and I ate it with a single-use plastic spoon.

I bought some grapes, too.
They came in a plastic zip-loc bag
with freshness breathing holes.

At home, I washed the grapes and put them in a bowl.
(The bowl was ceramic.)
I put the plastic grape bag on the counter
as a place to collect other plastic bags.
We finished a loaf of bread
and I put that bag in the collection bag.

I also unpacked all the Charmin rolls,
stacked them in the closet, and added their
scrunched-up plastic bags to the collection.

We received a mail-order delivery:
five feet of corrugated plastic tubing,
part of a dust collection system in our woodshop.

It came in a cardboard box sealed
with acrylic adhesive tape.
Inside the box, the tubing was wrapped
in plastic bubble wrap.

The bubble wrap was too bulky
to fit in the plastic grape bag on the counter
so I removed the biggest Charmin plastic bag
and made it the collection bag.

It was two o'clock in the afternoon.
I had driven twelve miles to Costco and back,
far short of the thousands of miles sailed
by Ahab and Ishmael, Starbuck and Stubb and Tashtego.
No harpoons or waif-poles,
no rope by the hundreds of fathoms,
yet I was already well on my way
to a whale's belly-load of plastic.

```
Rita Moe, Age 72
Roseville, MN
Writer / Weeder / Knitter
```

All Persons Should Breathe Clean Air

Throughout my practice of 34 years as an anesthesiologist, I noticed the increasing frequency of patients, young and old, using inhalers and experiencing respiratory distress when their inhalers didn't work. In 1980, during my second year of residency at the University of Minnesota, I was part of a team that used an extreme intervention to save a six-year-old girl with acute asthma. In 2017, during the wildfire season in the west, my own grandson had to be rushed to the emergency room when his asthma attack didn't respond to his inhaler.

Data shows that the amount of air pollution in Minnesota steadily increased through 2005; the Next Generation Energy Act, a bipartisan bill that was signed by Governor Tim Pawlenty in 2007, improved air quality for a while. However, Minnesota once again has hazardous air quality days, with high heat and ambient pollution from wildfires. The science is telling us that the number of these days will increase as climate change increases. Of great concern is that certain at-risk groups are especially vulnerable. The elderly, young, and poorer communities suffer disproportionately with hazardous air quality days.

I also am concerned about my grandchildren and all students who are exposed to air pollutants while they wait to board idling diesel buses. That's why I support Minnesota's plan of helping school districts to purchase electric school buses. With transportation now the largest emitter of climate-damaging pollution, it's time for immediate action.

The climate crisis is impacting so many aspects of public health. Besides air pollution, climate change is also making people more susceptible to heat stress, vector-born diseases, and mental health issues. A good friend of mine, aged 54, died of heat stroke while chopping wood on a hot, humid day in northern Minnesota. Another colleague suffers from chronic Lyme disease that she got from a tick bite while living through Hurricane Katrina. When I was a medical student in 1974, only a handful of Minnesota counties reported cases of Lyme disease. Today it is reported in every county.

A new mental health term was coined in 2005— "solastalgia"—which is a form of psychic or existential distress caused by environmental change close to home that causes loss and sadness. For some people, such as those whose homes and the entire region where they lived have been destroyed by fires or hurricanes, solastalgia can be all-encompassing. But climate change is causing solastalgia for many people. I have noticed these kinds of feelings in myself, such as when I can't enjoy being outdoors because it is too hot and humid and air quality is at a dangerous level. I am saddened when I can't cross-country ski because there is not enough snow. I also experience some underlying fear of going camping or going on our spring search for morel mushrooms due to deer ticks. I am distressed wondering what our grandchildren will face 60-80 years from now with climate change.

I am now retired but have realized that health professionals can play a large role in educating and advocating for the health of our fellow Minnesotans. I am a co-founder of Health Professionals for a Healthy Climate, a Minnesota non-profit, that has over 500 dedicated members who understand that the health crisis will only get worse without urgent action. The impact of climate change on the health of our patients is a climate emergency, and as physicians, we take very seriously the Hippocratic Oath which requires us to prevent what we cannot treat.

I am proud to stand with many health organizations calling for immediate action on this climate and health crisis. I stand for the people we care for, our children, the elderly, and the marginalized. It has been a privilege to practice medicine for 34 years and I will continue to advocate for the health of our Minnesota citizens.

```
Mike Menzel, MD, Age 70
Edina, MN
Physician / Grandparent / Climate Activist
```

Aftermath

Everything we cherish about life, whether it be the rich soil needed for us to grow vegetables and crops, the trees and plants that give us our oxygen, the clean water we all as human beings depend on to keep the blood flowing in our bodies—all of this will greatly be affected without our immediate intervention to slow or stop climate change. For this art piece, I wanted to use as many materials as possible found in nature, such as dirt, tree bark, and stones, to show that no matter how small or insignificant something may seem to you, everything in life serves a purpose.

Our planet is changing rapidly every day we choose to not act. We're taking our present for granted while not being cautious of a potentially grim future. There may come a time when we can no longer provide for ourselves—or more importantly, our families. Many already experience the pain of hunger with no ability to remedy it. Our clean air is now polluted; the water is now tainted with toxins. Mother Nature has no energy to defend herself. Our precious atmosphere eventually falls and unleashes those ultraviolet sun rays we were once protected from. The feeling of rainfall touching your body becomes a distant memory. A raging wildfire begins to devastate everything in its path, and all that will remain will be ashes.

Taji Joseph, Age 26
Minneapolis, MN
Visual Artist / African-American / Uncle

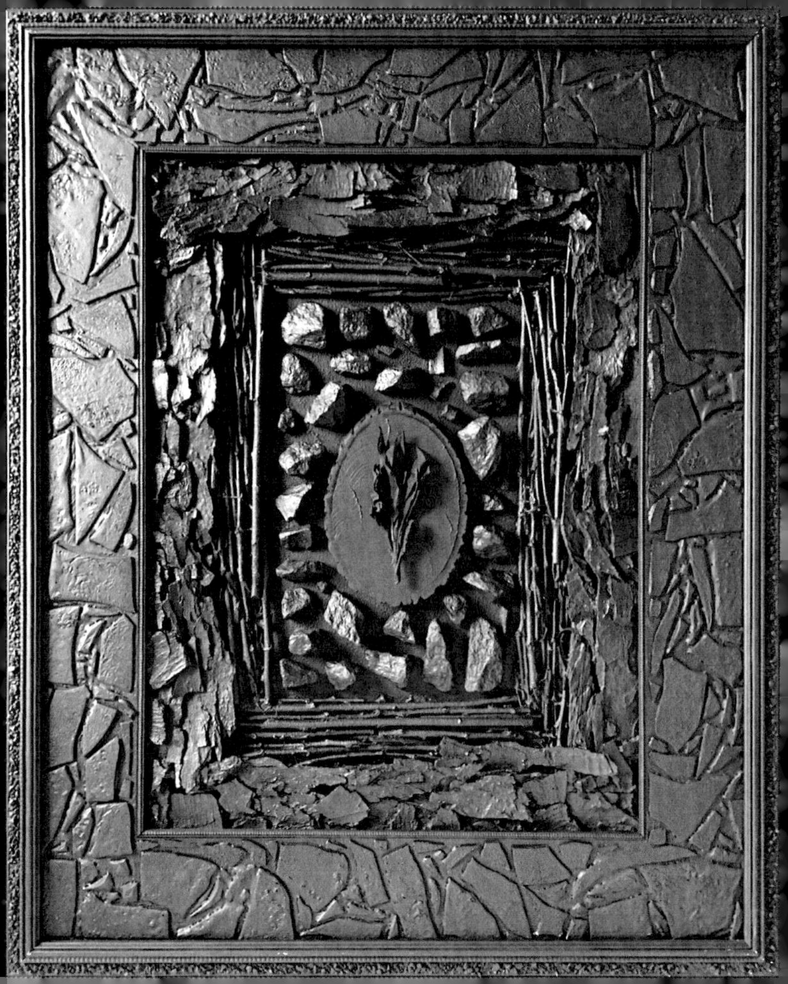

The Forgotten

My name is Izzy Laderman. I am 16 years old. I live in Duluth, Minnesota, and I am disabled.

With the climate crisis, it is my future—my generation's future—that is at stake. My generation will have to deal with the gases and pollution pumped into the atmosphere and destroying the Earth. Global warming is increasing the frequency and severity of natural disasters, and these disasters disproportionately harm people with disabilities.

Climate crisis movements must be intersectional. Too often, however, people with disabilities are left out. We have become what one writer calls "expected casualties" or "unpreventable losses," with even the people fighting the crisis frequently failing to remember us. We have become background characters in a movement that will leave us especially vulnerable.

By 2050, there will be at least 200 million people displaced by the climate crisis, according to the *Guardian*. Of those, 18 million will be people with disabilities. That number is expected to increase as catastrophes disable more people.

Minnesota, and especially my hometown of Duluth, is already being touted as a center for environmental refugees. *The New York Times* named Duluth one of the two cities in the United States—the other is Buffalo, New York—that will seem least affected by the climate crisis.

People are going to move here, and some of these people are going to have disabilities.

Is our federal government, which has done so little to mitigate the crisis, going to aid them? The government already falls short in the aid it provides to people with disabilities. It must start planning for how it can best provide assistance now. But it doesn't need to start from scratch. The government can turn to excellent work already done by organizations such as the World Institute on Disability.

People have already died. During Hurricane Katrina, a woman drowned in her home because she couldn't walk away to escape. I learned this story only when specifically looking up stories like these to help prove my point. Disabled deaths are only infrequently talked about. But disabled deaths can be prevented. The government must act.

Of course, as a disabled person living in Duluth, I am privileged. I am most likely not going to die during a natural disaster. I have family and friends to help me if a disaster were to occur. But not everyone has that privilege.

Too many people are already dead or are fighting for their lives while struggling with their health. I want to use my privilege to raise this issue, to make people aware that this is happening.

An intersectional movement must include those who are disabled, and the government must provide assistance. Too often we are ignored or marginalized.

We will not be silent.

I will not be silent.

```
Izzy Laderman, Age 16
Duluth, MN
Education Director for MN
Youth Climate Strike / White
and Filipina / Disabled
```

Waking Up

Climate change is an issue that affects literally everyone on the entire planet. I want to help get the word out about it and raise awareness. But at the same time I have to admit I also feel a little bit like a phony.

A couple of brief examples to paint the picture: I grew up pretty much hating camping and anything involving the great outdoors (although, in a strange twist, the movie *The Great Outdoors* with John Candy is def on my Top Five All-Time list). I've been given the nickname Towel Man due to the insane amount of napkins and paper towels that I use at each meal to clean my hands after every bite.

I've been a mixture of blissfully ignorant and bandwagon woke about most environmental causes—always quick to pat myself on the back when I do the slightest thing that might be considered environmentally conscious. Yes, I recycle. When the plastic straw issue rocked the world last year (or at least my social media bubble of the world), I bought metal straws for our house. Told everyone I knew about it—really hyped it up. I was actually recently replying to a *City Pages* email asking me what I do to help out the environment, and while I was launching into a full-on Metal Straw Warrior response I realized I had just used about 20 ziplock bags to pack my kids' lunches that morning. Oops.

I was recently asked to share my personal climate story, and I kind of had an existential crisis. To this point my climate story has been that I just assumed other people had all this shit figured out. And sure, the coasts will eventually fall into the ocean but here in beautiful Minnesota we're gonna be just fine.

Social media is a total gift and a curse, but one thing I've really appreciated about it is that I get to see so many personal stories from all over the world. And I'm seeing how climate change is truly impacting people everywhere on a daily basis, and seeing those personal stories allows me to feel empathy and realize that things are much bigger than me, and that there is not some magical force or government out in the world who's figuring this shit out.

A while ago I remember hearing about sea level rise, almost in a fantastical way. It felt like a movie. Like that movie *The Day After Tomorrow* (also a classic). Or that San Andreas film with Dwayne "The Rock" Johnson. This thing about the sea level rising and causing all sorts of problems was just a crazy summer blockbuster plot, not a real-life issue.

Now it seems like every person around the world has a story about "hey, things used to not be like this here when I was younger, but now there are extremely noticeable negative changes happening to my environment all around." I saw a video from someone in Scandinavia recently showing the actual effects of the ice caps melting and flooding into their rivers. And I swear, it didn't used to snow here in Minnesota eight months out of the year.

I think my climate story right now is that I'm just starting to wake up to the critical issues facing us all, and I'm honestly a bit groggy from a complete lifetime of ignorance and apathy. I do want to learn and I do want to change, but I don't totally know what to do or how to do it. So I guess that it's OK to not have this stuff totally figured out for yourself yet. We're all figuring it out together.

What I do know is that I can't be silent anymore. I can't just believe that someone else will sort out this problem. I want to learn more about climate change myself, about what I can personally do to get people connected. As a musician and a producer, I have a platform, no matter how big or small, to share my voice, and to open up a dialogue that matters.

And most importantly to say that what you do matters too, and you are not alone in this. Love to each and every single one of you out there.

Aaron "Lazerbeak" Mader, Age 37
Minneapolis, MN
Musician / Caucasian / Father

The Choice

In my relatively short life in public policymaking, I have been a part of three generations of change agents. In the 1960s we began to make real the promise of equal rights and equal justice for all Americans, especially those disadvantaged for centuries by poor health, disability, race or economic status.

By the time in the 1970s when I was elected to the U.S. Senate as a Republican from Minnesota, I brought with me from Minnesota a commitment to restoring and preserving natural resources.

During my third term in the Senate in the late 1980s and into the 1990s, I had the pleasure of helping a Republican president sign into law the bipartisan work on clean cir, clean water and natural resource preservation by a majority Democratic Senate and House of Representatives.

How was it possible? Colleagues of mine like Al Gore can be credited. But more important were my constituents in Minnesota.

Chief among them was Will Steger, whose teams of explorers and the stories of their Arctic treks I brought to Washington D.C., where they could meet presidents and their families. But more important, through national media, their discoveries of the real, live consequences of climate change were shared worldwide.

When I left the Senate after three terms in 1995, I left behind just one colleague whom we might call a "climate denier." Today, Republican Senator James Inhofe of Oklahoma has been joined by nearly every Republican member of Congress and Republican President Donald

Trump in denying the equal rights to a healthy climate of every American. These Republicans profess it is in our national interest to relieve industries of the burden we policymakers once asked them to undertake to reduce the public health consequences of their production. It was our commitment to the industry that all who benefit from clean energy will share the costs associated with cleaner fuels.

The end of bipartisan national policymaking in the name of limiting carbon dioxide production is another unconscionable burden that Americans are being asked to bear. Just one of the reasons people like me, who have been blessed to know better, have chosen to "retire" from the Republican Party.

David Durenberger, Age 85
Saint Paul, MN
Grandparent / Concerned Citizen / Retired Politician

Perspective From the Smokestack

I was born in the Bay Area and raised in Richmond, California, by two wonderful Mexican and Salvadoran immigrants. Richmond is a predominantly Black and Mexican community that is barely affordable for working class families living in the Bay Area. It is also home to the second largest oil refinery in the state of California.

As a kid, my friends and I always thought the refinery created clouds, since white smoke was always coming out of the smokestacks. We never thought of it as something dangerous and harmful. One day the refinery exploded and darkened the sky, sending many to the hospital with respiratory problems. After the explosion, I started to connect the dots about environmental discrimination.

I came to Minnesota to study Political Science, Latin American Studies, and American Studies at Macalester College. I did not personally feel the environmental discrimination, since I had the privilege to study at a liberal arts college in a well-resourced neighborhood of St. Paul. But I have listened to the stories of many people during my time at Macalester and since, as an environmental justice organizer with COPAL (Comunidades Organizado El Poder y La Acción Latina).

Many in the environmental movement in Minnesota and around the country understand we need to save the Boundary Waters and save the polar bears. Caring about the well-being of animals and nature is important in our fight for climate resilience and restoration. But it must be understood that racial and gender equity are huge and essential parts in our fight for environmental justice.

In my work as an organizer for environmental justice, I have met many people whose stories make it clear that many environmental injustices have happened and continue to transpire in Minnesota. Indigenous lands have been forcibly taken and are still being disrespected by oil companies encroaching on sacred lands. Pipelines are not job creators; they destroy nature and disrupt culture.

The Rondo community in St. Paul was a thriving Black community until highway planners decided to bulldoze it in the 1960s to make way for Interstate 94. A whole community was torn in half, the heart of it torn out, to accommodate more cars in the Twin Cities.

Currently, trash incinerators near poor Black, Indigenous, and communities of color in Minneapolis are continuously violating those residents' human right to clean air. As a consequence, many of our Minnesota residents in poor communities of color develop health problems that they can barely afford to treat. This is just what happened around the refinery in Richmond when I was a child.

Climate change is a threat multiplier, and the repercussions of it have been a central part of creating economic and environmental refugees in Latin America and around the world. Many come to the United States to escape brutal neoliberal policies and to find opportunity. Many come to find a place of refuge from land that has become dried out and unliveable because of climate change, but they are met with a system based in white supremacist ideologies that discriminates against them. Yet the responsibility of the U.S. towards Latin American immigrants is not acknowledged. Major fossil fuel companies with power and money are actively protecting their interests by funding political candidates who openly deny the science of climate change. When I lived in California, the Chevron Corporation tried to influence the city election in Richmond so the city would not fine them for polluting the air and allowing their refinery to explode.

A powerful woman named Berta Caceres, who worked for environmental justice in Honduras and was assassinated for it, once warned us, "Let us wake up, humankind! We're out of time. We must shake our conscience free from the rapacious capitalism, racism, and patriarchy that will only assure our own self-destruction."

The time is now to respect human lives and Mother Earth. We need to reject the colonizer ideology that we can manipulate nature to do our bidding, and that we can continue to burn fossil fuels, build pipelines and allow oil refineries to blow up with no consequences. We need to work in harmony with the land and respect people's space. Our land is sacred. We need to retain and restore our cultures and traditions. There is a lot to lose if we don't take bold action now for climate justice.

The time is now to switch from an extractive capitalist economy to a regenerative economy. A world where ecological and social well-being is the norm rather than enclosure of wealth and power. A world where we advance racial justice and social equity and where anti-blackness is no longer the foundation of our shared culture. A world where people and nature are protected and treated with care and justice.

```
Marco A. Hernandez, Age 22
Saint Paul, MN
Environmental Justice
Organizer / Mexican
Salvadoran / Large-hearted
```

I Carry the Grief of the World

And this is the condemnation: that Light is come into the world, and men loved darkness rather than light... JOHN 3:19

I carry the grief of the world
in a joyful body. What should I do?

At dawn, I step out of the door, pleased
to find the sun once again cool and friendly.

At evening, I retire to my hut
desperate and murderous, the
earth retiring in flames.

At midnight the moon mocks
monks who see in her brave shine
cool enlightenment, not hot despair.

Soon enough dawn will arrive
as the Devil himself striding
over the rim of the world,
horned head hot with laughter.

What witless pact we mortals signed
to gain the slaves toiling inside our dishwashers,
lighting our way at night, amusing us to sleep.

I already feel the heat, and the shame,
and it is not yet noon.

James P. Lenfestey, Age 75
Minneapolis, MN
Author / Concerned Citizen / Grandparent

From EARTH IN ANGER: 25 POEMS OF LOVE AND DESPAIR FOR PLANET EARTH, Red Dragonfly Press, © 2012. Used by permission of the author.

> "Endings are a linear construct and this story is a spiral."
>
> -Ben Weaver, pg.68

RESILIENCE

Disrupting the Binding

Two birds flew out from a cloud,
I looked up as they went overhead
feeling a tug between their bodies and mine
a triangle formed between us,
my heart the center point.

Hope is a form of poverty,
it is a thief of the present moment
creating debt by nurturing dissatisfaction,
promising something or someone or sometime
other than this, us and now.

As the two birds
flew into the distance
the strings between our bodies
stretched out like a slingshot.

I could no longer see them when it happened
but when the birds let go,
my eyes turned into the bottoms
of stones and I awoke
in the center of a glacier.

History depends on forms of repetition
repeating themselves and
the present moment
offers endless opportunity to
reorganize and disrupt that repetition.
This is what the wind
does with seeds,
the fox with their tracks
and the ocean with its rolling white teeth.

Eventually the glacier began to melt
and as my eyes softened a story emerged
that went something like this.

Collectively we overthrew
the cultural hierarchy
that had embedded our lives
in the destructive patterns and beliefs
that insisted on putting an addiction
for convenience and comfort
over the needs of rivers and butterflies,
viewing Mississippi and Walleye
as resources rather than relatives,
and asserting the word of adults was somehow
superior to the laughter of children.

Soon I was engulfed in cold singing water,
pools of it ran in the hollows of my shoulder,
all that remained of the glacier.

I could smell an ending,
like rain seeding the horizon,
but from here it didn't go
how you'd think it might go.

Endings are a linear construct
and this story is a spiral.

Two runaway horses
came up out of the river
and my breath filled with giant wings,
I could blow holes in the rain
and the rain also blew inside of me,
it washed out the poverty and sorrow
that had accumulated from so much hope.
I was not the only one that this happened to,
it was happening to all of us.

We built fires in the shadow spaces where ice had been,
called back by roses,
we planted trees into the uncertainty and loss,
we healed through our capacity to cooperate.

As we unbound ourselves from hope
our wills became feral and regrew tails.
The two birds turned around
and flew back and forth crossing in the sky
above where the horses stood,
their hooves dripping
the edge of the river
back into the river.

Though this is as far into the spiral as I am able to write,
the inherent wisdom of the surrounding land
stands strongly in their truth
and will speak, as much as one is willing to listen.

When I have placed my ear to their heart, I have heard them say,
"Lead with curiosity, the stories support the systems
and in turn the systems support the stories,
be aware which system and which story you support.
It is a trick of capitalism to shift shape
because its extractive nature
is happy to appear as a different form of energy
enabling itself to remain in control
managing the pace and direction of change
ensuring that nothing actually changes,
if in doubt return to your breath
it serves as a constant reminder of cooperation
if you give too much you die
if you take too much you die,
endings are a linear construct,
this story is a spiral,
be with the birds"

Ben Weaver, Age 40
Saint Paul, MN
Bike Wilder / Father / Poet

Bagosenim (Hope)

Three strands of sweetgrass, braided, entwined:
Wisdom, nurturance, love.
Indigenous women rise strong
Of this land, for this land,
For our future.
When Native voices lead,
There is resonance in the water, the air, the plants and creatures
So injured from centuries of exploitation and neglect.
Still, enduring.
Still, containing all the essential knowledge of resilience,
Revealed in Anishinaabe Kwe
Leading us forward, onward, to a restoration of social and environmental justice.
We are stewards of this place.
Sweetgrass, the long hair of Mother Earth, is a gift and a reminder
Of our duty
And the honor of following the path built by Indigenous women,
And the gift of hope
That our Earth will return to sacredness.

```
Katy Backes Kozhimannil, Age 41
Vadnais Heights, MN
Guardian / Professor / Mother
```

Clearer Waters

Minnesota truly is the land of 10,000 lakes, and I am currently on an expedition to explore as many as I can. Water is life. My connection to our natural world has fueled my passion for the environment and has led me to protect what I love. I started an environmental club at my high school and spoke as a panelist at my local town hall, and I express my motivation to care about climate change through art. Nature is where I truly feel the most at home, and I am willing to protect it at all costs.

Jasmine Dawn Holt, Age 17
Maple Grove, MN
Asian American / Student Activist / Avid Naturalist

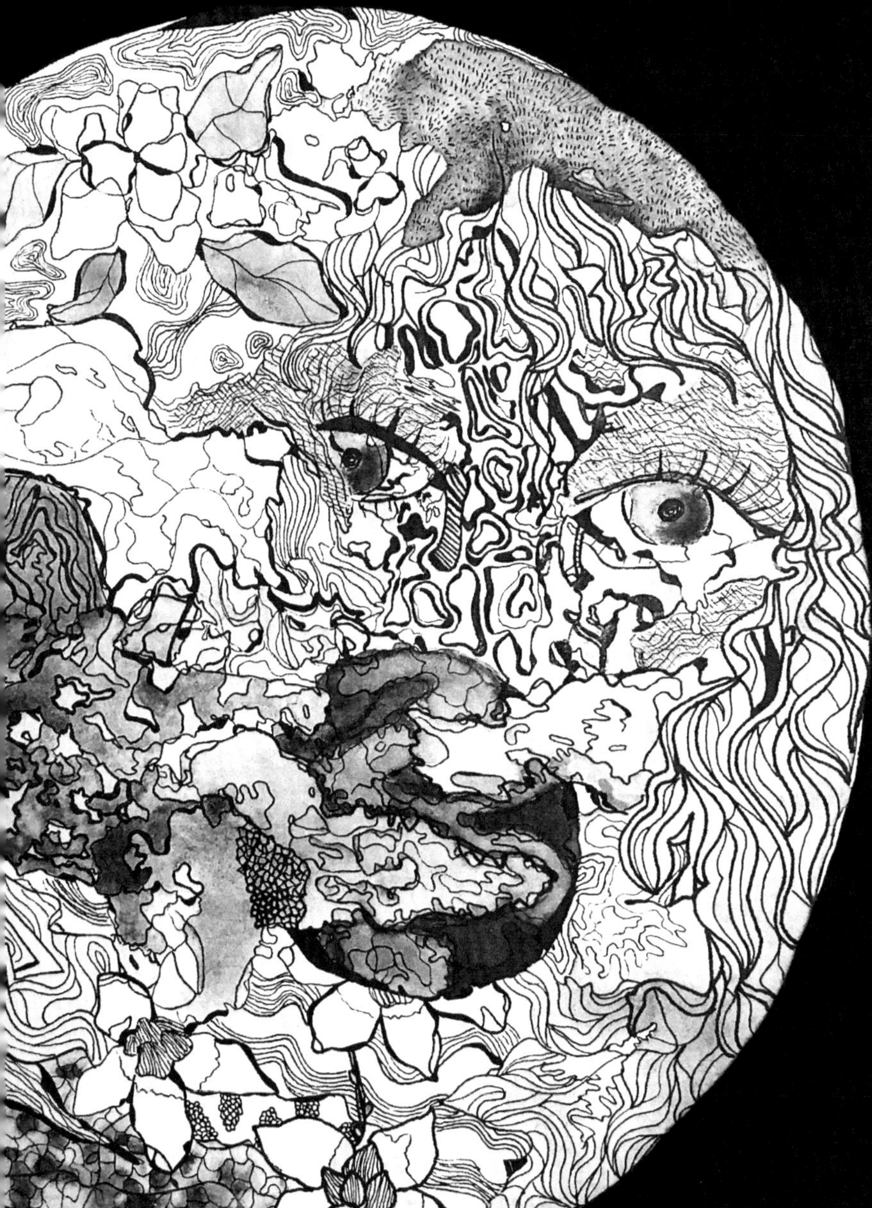

Opening My Eyes

If I'm being honest, I'd never really thought about climate change before. It always seemed like a big task, something to just leave up to politicians. I'm only a teenager.

I realized that I was wrong.

I visited my family in Ethiopia and Somalia during the summer of my freshman year in high school. It didn't click for me that my family struggled financially, not having enough money to buy food or clothing for themselves. My aunt would slaughter goats and sheep and make celebratory meals for us that were only for special occasions. Despite having very little, my family was still very grateful for all that they had.

Two years after my visit, a drought hit Somalia. More than 2.9 million people have been affected by the drought since 2017. There was a big famine, killing most livestock, including all of my family's animals. There was nothing to eat, only unclean water to drink, and diseases like measles and cholera began to spread. My people were dying.

I can't say absolutely that this drought was due to climate change. But I know that climate change has played an influential role in making weather more extreme. Because of our fossil-fuel society, there will be more droughts, more floods, more hurricanes—not just in other places around the world, but right here in Minnesota, too.

I have realized that the little things I do matter, like talking to my friends about climate change. And I know I can do big things, too. In 2018 I helped to organize a summit of 100 youth to meet with Governor Dayton and lawmakers, to urge them to fight for climate justice. Doing something like that had always seemed impossible for me.

Climate change is significant in our lives whether we realize it or not. It is time that we open our eyes to the suffering of others and understand the weight of the reality that we all face. We need to realize that it is not enough to have compassion; there must also be action.

```
Munira Berhe, Age 19
Minneapolis, MN
She-Her / Voter / First Generation
```

Uncovering Rondo

When I think about community, I think about a group of people active in addressing injustices even if those injustices only impact a few members of that community. Growing up, it was just me and my mom as I was an only child. We moved to the Midway/Rondo area when I was four or five years old. My mom was the kind of person who liked to foster that sense of community; she was a big part of making our new home feel like a neighborhood for me. When I came home from school she would often be visiting our neighbors, talking and sharing snacks in their backyard.

We were close to our next door neighbors at the time—we would often help each other out with things such as pet-sitting or lending tools. Visiting people in our community gave me a feeling of comfort, trust, safety, and connectedness. These experiences have strongly shaped the importance of seeking to build connections in my world, to find people to be in close proximity with, and to have deep and mutually beneficial relationships.

For me, the Rondo community is home. When I attended St. Paul Central High School, I would cross over Interstate 94 every day to get back home from school. I couldn't help but notice that things were different on the two sides of the freeway. Rondo seemed like a community that was fractured, yet healing. I could perceive deep communal roots in the area, but I also detected a sense of disconnection between those roots and reality.

I noticed over time that smaller businesses would tend to come and go as if it was difficult to maintain consistent business. There were more and more chain restaurants and fast food restaurants along University Avenue. If I didn't want a quick and easy bite to eat, I would have to go to Marshall Avenue, or beyond. Even though there were more white people and retail stores in that area, I got more of a complete sense of community on that side as there were newer parks, a community center, and spaces for people to interact with one another. I remember wishing

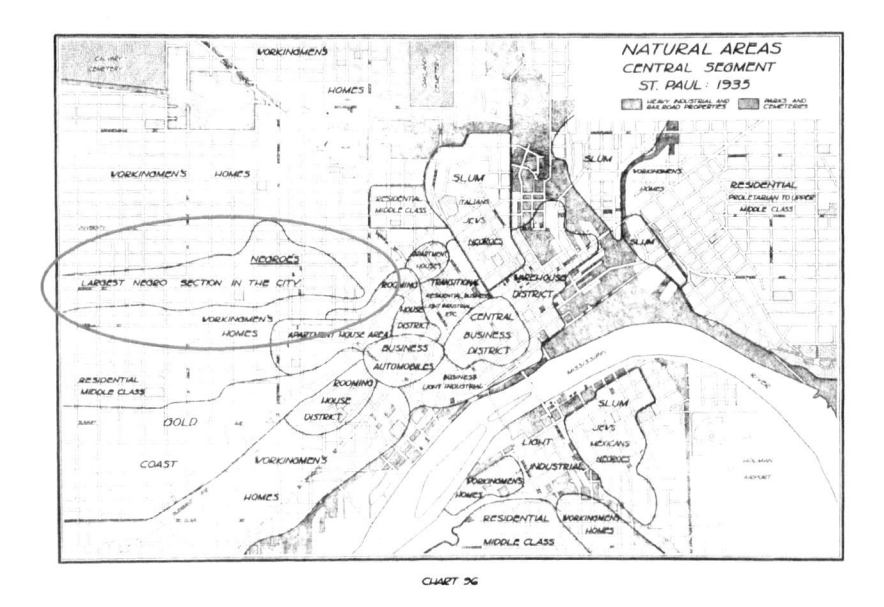

Image Credit: Social Saga of Two Cities: an Ecological and Statistical Study of Social trends in Minneapolis and St. Paul by Dr. Calvin Schmidt (2002)

that I didn't have to go so far away from my neighborhood to feel that sense of community.

During my college years, I learned that racialized oppression has deep intersections with the issue of climate change, and found that the development of I 94 was largely responsible for why my neighborhood was struggling. The development of I 94 fractured the predominantly Black community of Rondo and placed an inexcusable environmental burden upon the community, resulting in severe repercussions for the health and culture of Rondo residents that are still being felt to this day.

One of the most informative resources I found was Dr. Calvin Schmidt's work, *Social Saga of Two Cities: an Ecological and Statistical Study of Social trends in Minneapolis and St. Paul*. In his study, Schmidt details the many attempts to segregate Rondo, the largest African-American community in the Twin Cities at the time. Efforts openly working for segregation proved unsuccessful, as laws at the time prohibited explicit segregation. In order to work around these laws, urban planners plotted to build I-94 directly through the community of Rondo to unofficially segregate the neighborhood.

As I researched, I began to put together my own experiences growing up with what I was learning, and that put it all into context for me. I realized that this blatant act of racism is an environmental injustice because the pollutants from the freeway not only contribute to climate change, but also inflict slow violence upon the health of the predominantly Black community of Rondo.

These realizations resulted in intense emotions. I felt sad and upset learning about how a community I lived so close to had been so adversely affected by systemic oppression. In contrast to that dismay, I also felt a sense of urgency. I had already started going to protests and getting involved in actions around environmental justice. Through these experiences I witnessed what collective power can look like, and what is possible when we show up together.

I see that intersection of environmental concern with social justice concern within my own sense of community. Learning about the history of the community I grew up in has been important to my own identity, and has reinforced a passion for environmental justice. It made it personal for me, as relationship building is one of the core foundations of how I do environmental justice work.

One of the impacts I hope to have through my work is to help cultivate that sense of community my mother showed me growing up. I truly believe that the more connected we are as individuals, the more our capacity for change grows.

Akira Yano, Age 22
Saint Paul, MN
Community Member / Environmental Justice Educator
Japanese-American

Bedtime Stories of the Khmer Americans

Bopha

Once upon a time there was a little girl living in a dark point in history, a time of turmoil and suffering. She was taught to hide, run, and survive from the age of 12. When she hid under the rotting flesh of her people, covered with mud from head to toe, she would dream of the peaceful time when she would go catch crawfish in the rainstorm and play with the ghost children in the cemetery.

Each day was the same—praying that the pile of dirt she stepped on wasn't a landmine, the rustling in the bushes was a lost dog and not a soldier, and every time she let go of her mother's hand that it wouldn't be the last time she felt her touch. The girl didn't know what her future would hold, and she never had time to think of it. Every time she woke at night, she had to survive the day.

Once upon a time there was a mother living in a home she never thought she'd have. She escaped the destruction of her country to come here—the home of the winter spirit of Minnesota.

The mother digs deep into the soil of her garden, planting her cucumber seeds and chili peppers, trying to grasp the familiarity of her farm back home. She cooks rich, flavorful meals for her family, using the hot chili peppers from the garden. The spice is nostalgic. That hot, burning sensation on the tongue brings her back to her mother's num banh chok recipe when she was sick as a girl.

Her life in Minnesota is meaningful and happy, but she will forever wonder if her home is still standing, if the stream behind her farm still flows, and if the spirit of her childhood still exists in the wind. The scariest question of all, the thought she tries so hard to hide—will the blood of indifference forever taint the ground that is home? Is there even a home to go back to?

Choup

Once upon a time there was a little boy living in a dark point in history, a time of turmoil and suffering. He was taught to work, obey, and survive from the age of three. The boy was forced out of his home, his family leaving everything behind and trying their hardest to keep the boy and his siblings alive. His parents worked long hours, miles away from the camp, leaving his siblings to fend for themselves.

The boy's sister became sick, getting skinnier and skinnier every week until he had to rest his head on her bones. The boy was starving, only getting small portions of salt and rice soup. The boy looked up at the starry night from the small hut his father built between the trees of the forest. That sky was all he'd ever known and the stars seemed so far as he counted how many stars away were his father and mother. The feeling of loneliness and exhaustion filled his small, tired body. Everytime he woke at dawn, he prayed for his mother and father to return by dusk.

Once upon a time there was a father living in a home he never thought he'd have. He escaped the destruction of his country to come here—a place that worships the spirit of shimmering snow and tall pines. A home he didn't choose, but soon he fell in love with the land, Minnesota's land. The father grew up here. The tragedy of Cambodia is something equivalent to those distant memories—the memories he can't quite put his finger on, but they sit there, scratching at the back of his head.

To him, the campgrounds of the North and the freshwater lakes are his true childhood. It's what made the father feel alive. He always craves new adventures, wanting to climb the tallest bluffs, ski down the steepest hill, and bike through the skinniest of trails. The father radiates the energy of Minnesota, an energy that if you took it away, he'd be left only with the memories of the defenseless, helpless little boy from the camp. A boy who was incapable of dreaming. Minnesota brought him back to life, allowing him to finally dream.

Liz

Once upon a time there was a daughter who was born in the great state of Minnesota, the first generation of the Khmer Americans. The spirit of the winter and adventure of the summer allowed her to thrive throughout her childhood. She lived in a home full of culture, tradition, and curiosity. She was taught to love, to be grateful, and celebrate who she was since birth.

The great outdoors taught her more about life than the warmth and coziness of the fireplace inside. As a little girl, the heaviest snowstorms sparked a curious fire in her eyes; she was determined to strap on her protective armour and build a snow kingdom beneath the pine tree in her backyard. In the summer, she woke up at the crack of dawn from her tent, raced to the docks, tackle box and fishing rod in hand, ready to catch the biggest one of them all. It was these experiences, the memories that inspire the daughter to take care of the land she calls home, the home where her parents survived and thrive.

Hearing the bedtime stories of times past has driven her compassion to fight for social and climate justice and for the freedom of others. The daughter spends the rest of her life ensuring that no one feels alone, that even though the world feels dark and hopeless, she would be the light for those suffering. The girl spends 100 years spreading love to strangers, and never stops using her voice. When she wakes, she marches with hope, and when she sleeps, she dreams of peace.

She stands with the Earth. She stands with her home.

```
Liz Lat, Age 21
Minneapolis, MN
Art Student / Cambodian American / First Generation
```

Solid Spiral

This is the parking ramp spiral at the Minneapolis Saint Paul (MSP) International Airport. The spiral represents our rising temperatures and how the data has climbed over time, while the cement structure represents the growing heat island effect of urban sprawl in metro areas. However, the parking ramp at MSP Airport also demonstrates a valuable and viable solution to climate change: it is home to the largest solar farm in the state of Minnesota. The 4.3 megawatt solar array on top of the MSP Airport parking ramp has generated almost eight million kilowatt hours of electricity since November 2015.

```
David Joel Riviera, Age 42
Minneapolis, MN
Photographer / Climate Activist / Son
```

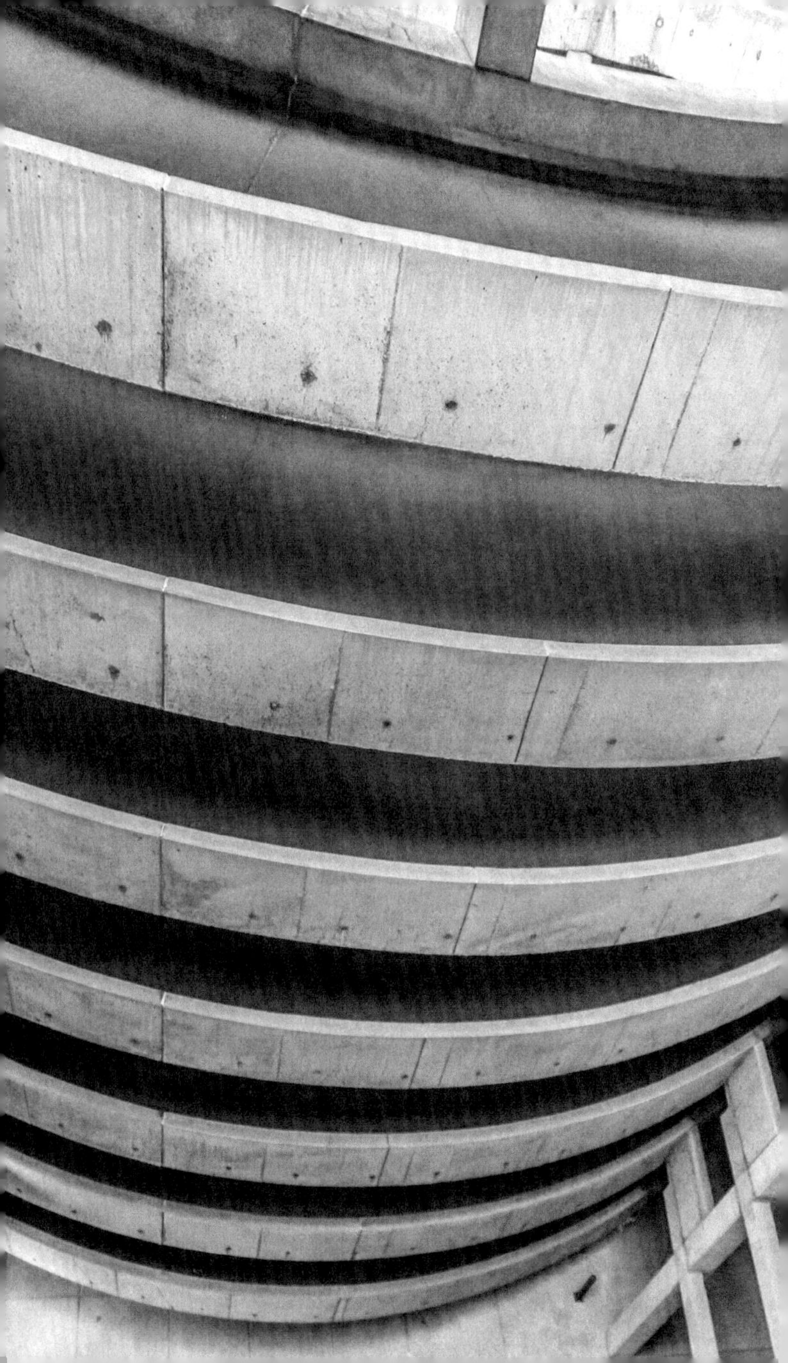

Breathe

A friend of mine showed me a YouTube video of satellite images of the ebbs and flows of Earth's ice-caps over the last few years. The Earth appears to breathe, just as we do. Inhales draw snow-covered landscapes toward the poles for warmer seasons, and exhales draw them to cover larger areas for the winter months.

As the video moved forward in time, the depth of the Earth's breaths became shortened, the snow and icescapes not flowing as far down as they used to. Their retreat cycles to the northern and southern poles were quickened like a human hyperventilation episode. I felt the tightness of the constriction of the Earth's cycle. This we know is attributable to global warming's climate changes, large polar ice masses are melting at alarming rates.

According to the National Aeronautics and Space Administration's (NASA) Gravity Recovery and Climate Experiment, "Greenland lost an average of 286 billion tons of ice per year between 1993 and 2016, while Antarctica lost about 127 billion tons of ice per year during the same time period. The rate of Antarctica ice mass loss has tripled in the last decade."

My mother, a 60-year old woman, fierce and strong, has started to have breathing problems from working in a taconite mine on the Iron Range of northern Minnesota. I've cried watching her struggle to catch her breath sometimes. Yet she adapts and powers on.

It was easy for me to draw the connection of the Youtube video of the planet to the experience of my mother, the struggle in fighting for deeper breaths, and in feeling so seemingly helpless at their receding patterns. The impact of this on me is pain, which wants to lead me to despair.

Yet I see my mother fighting to sustain herself, until the end of her days. I imagine Mother Earth is fighting in the same way, and so they together are teaching me to remain resilient in the face of change, to accept responsibility and face it bravely. There is still so much we can do to support the Earth's changes. We just have to find our connection and empathy to access motivation. I pray we all find it soon.

Miigwech (Thank you)

Dani Pieratos, Age 31
Lake Vermillion Reservation, MN
Mother / Business Owner / Indigenous

Stop Global Warming
_____

The sun, the wind and the people: it takes all kinds of power to make things move. Created for the Climate Crisis Coalition of the Twin Cities. (2006)

Ricardo Levins Morales, Age 63
Minneapolis, MN
Artist / Puerto Rican / Organizer

STOP GLOBAL WARMING

WITH NATURAL ENERGY AND GRASSROOTS POWER

CLIMATE CRISIS COALITION OF THE TWIN CITIES

Family Stories of the Past Give Insight to the Future

The depiction of a white picket fence charred at the top and submerging at the bottom is a reference to images on the news media I saw in the flooding stories of Hurricanes Irene, Lee and Sandy that battered the East Coast, including New York. These weather events were ultimately responsible for my 73-year-old father-in-law losing his home in Binghamton, New York, after its entire downtown was flooded. During these events, a poignant image of a picket fence submerged around the perimeter of a house reminded me of my father-in-law's home.

Next, the fires of California filled the media with images and again I saw a white picket fence in the foreground of a raging house fire. It jolted my memory of an exhibit at the Hinckley Fire Museum in Minnesota about the Great Hinckley Fire of 1894, where one of the only things not burned to the ground in the city of Hinckley was a piece of a white picket fence. As I was constructing an art installation at the time entitled "The New Climate" with burned pine trees, I was inspired to connect the dots on how human-caused environmental disasters from the past are lessons for the future. The painting "Phoenix Fence of Fire And Floods" was created.

```
MaryBeth Hoover Garrigan, Age 62
Saint Paul, MN
Mother / Artist / Eagle Whisperer
```

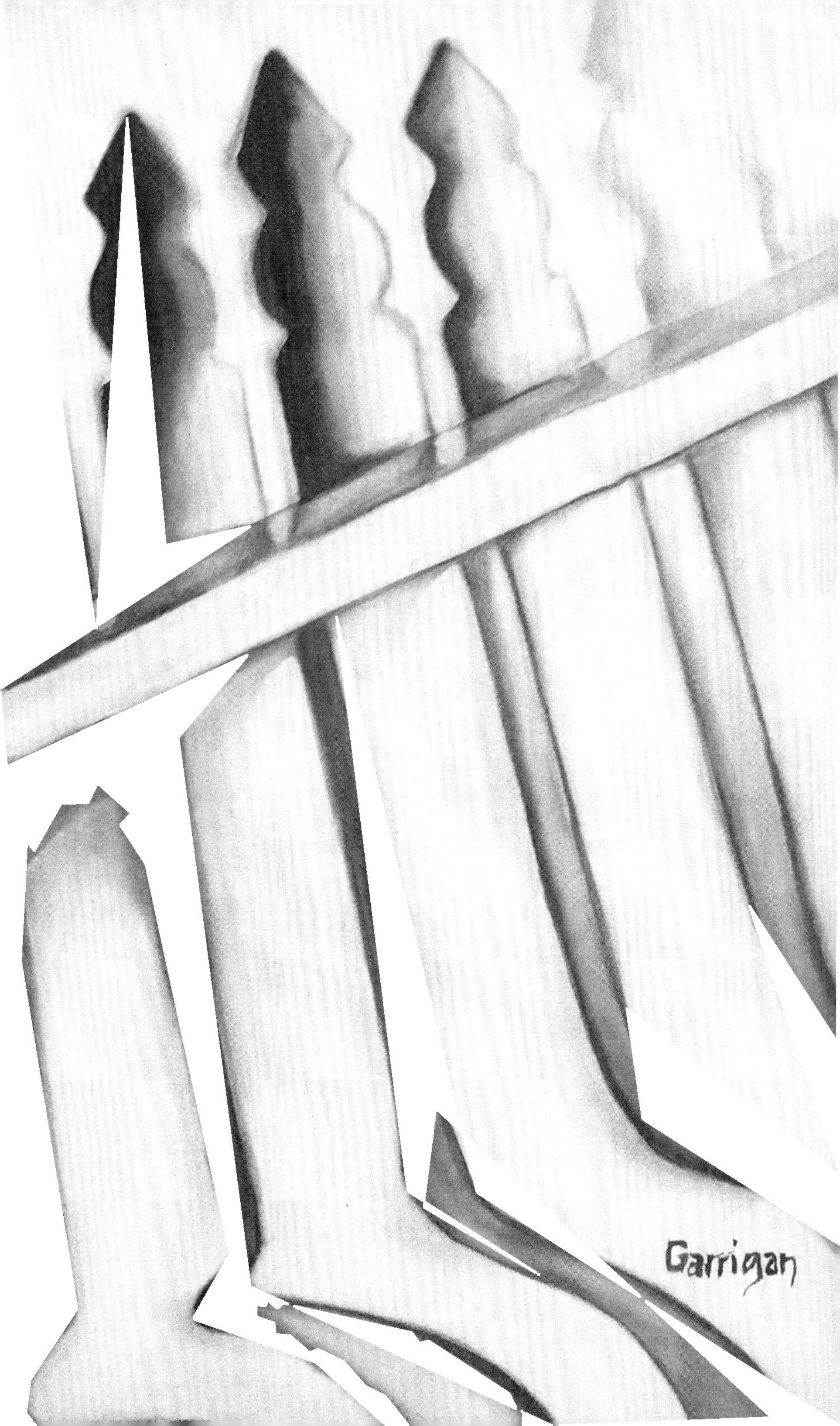
Garrigan

"We who can affect change in the physical world have a responsibility to leave the world a better place not only for the billions of humans who are still our potential descendants, but for the future generations of all living things. And though the outlook is often bleak, I have reasons for hope."

-Jeremy Messersmith, pg.93

HOPE

No Spoilers

I have a confession:

I'm a terrible person.

I read the last page of every book first.

And I only bother to even read a book so I can spoil the upcoming TV show. I love spoilers. I can't help it. As a kid, there was barely a Christmas or birthday that went by without complete foreknowledge of the presents. I would rifle through notebooks and snoop through closets looking for clues and unwrapped gifts. It's a deep character flaw; a symptom of a fragile and brittle mind. For me, not knowing is pure agony. I can't bear tension and I hate surprises. So I spoil everything and I live my life by the words of Oscar Wilde, who said: "The only way to get rid of temptation is to yield to it."

With fiction it's often easy to predict what's going to happen, thus resolving the tension. The protagonist wants something, and by the end they get it, usually through some kind of heroic sacrifice. I like to think I'm pretty good at predicting a film based solely on the trailer. But tension in real life is not so easily or neatly resolved, which brings me to the big knot of our time: climate change. Here's the movie trailer version as best I can understand it.

We live in a new age—the Anthropocene, an age where human activity is now the dominant influence on climate and the environment. We have marked this era with fallout from nuclear weapons, soot from power plants, concrete and micro plastics—our humble contributions to the geological record. It's an age of mass extinction with 75% of all species on Earth set to die out over the next 200 years. Increasing carbon dioxide in the atmosphere is causing extreme weather and rising sea levels. The degradation of our environment now threatens our very existence. We are in the midst of global ecocide.

That, my friends, is some supremely dark shit. I don't know about you, but it makes me want to find a nice beach somewhere and bury my head firmly in the sand. It's too much sorrow to process, the problem too big to comprehend. It's paralyzing. How do you mourn a planet? What song can I possibly sing for all my fellow creatures forever silenced?

Some may find solace in a holy book or a holy bottle. I say great, whatever helps you get through the day is fine by me. But for me? Well, being the weak-minded person I am, I need to know how it all ends. Luckily, there is a place that has all the juicy spoilers I so desperately crave.

It's a Wikipedia page titled "Timeline of the far future." I start near the end.

At an entry labeled "7.59 billion years from now" I find the following comfort (spoiler alert): "The Earth and Moon are very likely destroyed by falling into the Sun."

Ahh, truly a balm for the soul.

Three billion years from now I find this ray of sunshine: "There is a roughly 1-in-100,000 chance that the Earth might be ejected into interstellar space by a stellar encounter before this point, and a 1-in-3-million chance that it will then be captured by another star. Were this to happen, life, assuming it survived the interstellar journey, could potentially continue for far longer."

Hot diggity dog. I'm no expert in statistics, but I believe a 1 in 3 million chance is far better than no chance.

Two billion years from now the oceans evaporate.
Eight hundred million years from now all the plants die.
Ten million years from now is the estimated time of a full recovery of biodiversity after the current extinction.

Now, you may be wondering what kind of psychopath finds comfort in the thought of the Earth falling into the sun. Fair enough. I guess it reminds me that while it's pretty much the end of the story (fade to black, roll the credits) it's not the end of my story. I have a remarkable superpower right now that I won't have in seven billion years: I'm alive. Most people aren't. The overwhelming majority of humans who have ever lived are dead, and though we can hear their echoes, they no longer sing to us.

It's us, the living, who wield this superpower in the physical world. And if Spiderman has taught me anything, it's that with great power comes great responsibility. We who can effect change in the physical world have a responsibility to leave that world a better place not only for the billions of humans who are still our potential descendants, but for the future generations of all living things. And though the outlook is often bleak, I have reasons to hope.

For the first time in human history, we have begun to see the Earth as the fragile, finite and delicately interconnected orb it is.

For the first time we can organize on a truly global scale.

And for the first time we have the ability to shape our world with tools our predecessors could never dream of.

I have spent and will spend the vast majority of time benched on the galactic sidelines. What a joy to be in the game! Alive. Here. Now. In the thick of it. Yet I know that I am able to do something about it.

Now I may know what happens on the very last page, but my chapter, the little one I write in every day, is still unfinished. And in this one very specific case, I think I'm much happier not knowing how it ends. So to all the fortune tellers and time travelers out there:

Please, no spoilers.

```
Jeremy Messersmith, Age 40
Minneapolis, MN
Musician / Human / Obscene Optimist
```

Bridges

I imagine a world where I don't have to worry about climate change. I imagine more bridges to connect us all, and more places to meet and play.

Aajay Harris, Age 6
Woodbury, MN
Awesome / Black-Asian / Kid

Excerpts from Oral Testimony to the House Select Committee on the Climate Crisis

In 2007, I testified to the Select Committee on Energy Independence and Global Warming. At that time I stated, "One of the most famous American industrialists of the 20th Century, Henry J. Kaiser, once observed 'Problems are just opportunities in work clothes.'" Twelve years later, I'm pleased to report that millions of Americans have put on their work clothes and got about the business of solving climate change.

Today, of the 6.7 million Americans who work in the energy and energy efficiency industries, more than 3.5 million or 50% are contributing to a lower emissions economy. More than 350,000 of them do this in the wind and solar energy industries, another 63,000 thousand in nuclear power plants, 66,000 in hydro, 70,000 in low emissions advanced natural gas generating plants, and thousands of others in geothermal, combined heat and power, battery storage and many other technologies.

If it is done right, with the interests of America's middle class and working families at heart, there will be a place at the table, a job, and a paycheck for every American while we solve the climate crisis. But we have to do it right.

```
David A. Foster, Age 71
Iron Range, MN
Labor Leader / Caucasian / Bridge Builder
```

Fireflies

Warm summer nights
Brought unexpected treasures
For little brown girls
Who dreamed of fairies and
Magic.
Twirling in nightgowns
Grass between their toes
Reaching for dancing lights
Dropping like amber
Jewels
In the dark.
Has that hope for
Magic
Disappeared?
Or have those jewels that dance in the twilight
Escaped to other worlds
Where brown girls dare to dream?

Robyne Robinson, Age 58
Minneapolis, MN
African American Arts Consultant / Patron / Journalist

Essay on Delivery of My Boys

In the dream of the boys before I knew I was pregnant, they ran across an open field in bright sunlight. I chased them through the tall prairie grass. One of them turned to me and said, "We deserve our own names."

I woke up from that dream and felt the heat of my womb in the dark of our bedroom, in the echo of a police siren crying across the night.

In Hmong we say that life is welcomed at the gate of death. After I safely delivered my boys, I saw that the round clock in the operating room was not moving, despite the movement of the people around me. I asked my attending nurse, Jen, "Am I going to die?" She answered, her hand to my forehead, "No, sweetheart, the hard part is done."

I checked the round clock on the white wall once more to see that the hands of time had indeed stopped for me. I asked Jen for two cups of warm water to send me off to the other side. I drank the water, savoring its heat in my mouth, feeling it travel down my throat into that area where my boys had been that was now empty. The nurses cleaned me up. They wheeled me out of the operating room. In the bright hallway, my mother ran toward me. I saw the relief in her eyes. I felt the light pressure of her hand on my heart. I watched as her eyes grew large and frantic. My heart stopped beating. I coded.

I woke up hours later in the Intensive Care Unit. I listened for the cries of my babies. Instead, I heard the words of my mother, sitting at the foot of my bed, her head bowed as she bartered for my life with her own. I ventured far to welcome my sons into this world: Thayeng, whose name means Peace in Hmong, my language, and Yuepheng, whose name means Freedom.

Of all the things that I wish for this Earth, I wish for peace and freedom. A refugee child from the wars of Southeast Asia, a young girl growing up in Minnesota's impoverished neighborhoods looking toward the hidden suns in the books I checked out from the library for a new dawn to rise, I never imagined what the rise of a new sun would reveal.

I've always known that the world was imperfect—as are we, mere mortals holding to life and each other, in the limited space and time we've been granted by the mercy of those around us. I learned of many of the wars that we've waged in the name of colonialism, of capitalism, of greed. I, like many in this world of 7.7 billion, am only learning about the costs of these wars—not only for the human race, but the entirety of life in this world as we know it.

In early spring, Freedom and Peace race each other across the spread of green lawn dotted with yellow blooms of dandelions. Freedom is ahead and Peace follows. They climb up high. They slide down low. They laugh and frolic in the open air. When I reach them, they run into my arms and tell me, "We belong to you, and to each other." They spread their arms wide and proclaim, "We belong to the world."

My heart, a mother's heart, aches for the world that they belong to even as it rejoices for a world that will know their laughter and their tears, the feel of their feet, the touch of their hands, the distance they represent between the past and future.

The past they come from is a confrontation of powers, of people, of places. The future does not appear so different.

I raise my voice with all these others in the hopes that there will be a future—no matter its imperfections—for Freedom and Peace to flourish and flower. I urge the people with power to choose life for all instead of life for just some; to make a declaration that we, as the human race, will commit to fostering gentler, less destructive living; that we will be kinder to a world that affords us life—even as we venture to the gates of death; that what they do and what we do will grant us salvation in the arms of the young who believe, who continue to believe, that belonging to us and the world is a beautiful, blessed thing.

Kao Kalia Yang, Age 38
Saint Paul, MN
Writer / Refugee / Parent

When I am Feeling Overwhelmed
___

It's easy to feel depressed and paralyzed by news about the ongoing climate crisis, and yet we can't take productive action while we cower in fear. For the past two years, I've been practicing disarming complicated and oppressive feelings (like anxiety and anger) by doing simple things; I hope one or two of these help you.

Lisa Troutman, Age 36
Saint Paul, MN
Illustrator / Mash-up / Engaged Citizen

When I am feeling overwhelmed by the sheer gravity of our evolving climate reality, I...

APPLAUD SOMEONE ELSE'S PLANET-FRIENDLY ACTION

Thank you! *Great idea!*

LEARN about HISTORY • GARDEN with less WATER • HOW to BUILD for EFFICIENCY • COMPOST 101

REMIND MY REPRESENTATIVES that I CARE.

STATE CAPITOL • CITY GOVT. • HOUSE of CONGRESS • U.S. SENATE

SCIENCE is REAL!!! PLEASE VOTE accordingly

SAVOR GOODNESS that still exists & REMEMBER what's come before

BREATHE DEEPLY & remember that:

EVERY ONE of us NEEDS EVERY ONE of us ♥

our ONLY CONSTANT is CHANGE

TALK CLIMATE because our STORIES & EXPERIENCES are IMPORTANT

when I was growing up, we... *YES! I remember...*

Feel INSPIRED to TAKE ACTION & WORK for EARTH JUSTICE!

EYEWITNESS | 100

The (Potential) Speed of Change

In the summers, while my parents worked during the day, my sister and I were looked after by a grandmotherly figure from our church.

Her name was Frances.

I must have been about nine years old the day Francis proudly took us to her car and showed us her newly installed CAR phone.

We were in awe: Wow. A phone you can talk on IN THE CAR! You didn't even have to be home to answer the phone: you could be out driving around somewhere and still be connected to people!

She wouldn't let us pick it up: it was too precious. And what she said will always stick with me. "Just imagine! When you grow up, ALL cars will have car phones."

In my work today, at the Minneapolis College of Art and Design, I'm a graphic designer and educator, and I help non-expert audiences better understand complex scientific issues like the climate crisis. I'm struck by the need for us to move quickly—really quickly—to ensure the survival of our species.

The latest science suggests that we really only have about ten years left to make a major shift in the way we live, work, travel, and do business.

Ten years.

In ten years, I will be almost 50, and my daughter will be 16.

So when I feel overwhelmed by the gravity of the climate crisis (which I do feel quite a lot), I imagine this scenario. I imagine my daughter a mere 10 years from now, looking back and laughing at what I am telling her today, when I say, like Francis, "Just imagine! When you grow up, ALL our energy will be from renewables."

I hope she'll laugh because in that future it will be preposterous to imagine that we were ever at this confused and questioning moment that we're currently in. I hope that by then, we will have leap-frogged into a world where all energy comes from renewables and climate change is being reversed: a future that would positively amaze us all over again through the rapid pace of technology, and innovation.

I know it's within the capabilities of us humans.

So in addition to the hard work we are all doing to keep the climate crisis from reaching a dangerous tipping point, the thing that gives me hope is to remember moments about how quickly change CAN happen, as I have seen in my lifetime.

```
Arlene Birt, Age 39
Minneapolis, MN
Visual Storyteller / Educator / Artist
```

Love and Loss: A Pond Hockey Story

Growing up in Minnesota, winter for me meant playing hockey. Walking to the local rink and skating with my friends on weeknights for maybe an hour or two. Saturdays and Sundays meant skating for four or five hours. All of this skating was done on outdoor ice in Cottage Grove.

In 1972, my family moved to Red Wing over Thanksgiving vacation. The following Monday, I started at a new school and didn't know any of my sophomore classmates. That first day, though, I found out hockey practice started that week. So, it was early December and we were back on the ice. I quickly met my new teammates, some of whom became lifelong friends. One in particular, our goalie, was the best man in my wedding, and I was the best man in his. We didn't know it then, but we were fortunate to be able to practice and play our entire season outdoors, keeping good ice from early December into March.

Over the years, I have witnessed the Red Wing community grow and change in ways I never would have imagined. Now outdoor ice is a rarity in southern Minnesota. One month, maybe five weeks, is now about all you can hope for when it comes to outdoor ice. Working with the Red Wing Public Works Department, I know this firsthand. In December, our crews work around the clock, if and when the temperatures are cold enough, to get the outdoor ice ready so the kids can go skating over Christmas vacation. Even if they do get ice by late December, the fear is that we will see another year with a January thaw bringing 40-degree temperatures and melting all of the ice.

For me, and many people my age, outdoor ice rinks were a major part of life in the winter. Minnesota has the nickname "The State of Hockey." Kids like me were called "Rink Rats." Hockey has always been a part of my life: playing, coaching, reffing, and for the last 35 years my wife and I have been minor officials for the Red Wing High School Boys' Hockey Team. But, the players are different now. They play indoors. No one in southern Minnesota counts on outdoor ice even for practices, and kids today don't know what being a "Rink Rat" means. For me, it is a sad reality that the weather is just too warm to support outdoor skating anymore.

It's not just quality ice that we are losing; the warmer winters are affecting our communities, too. The Red Wing City Council had to make a very difficult decision several years ago. Making ice is a time-consuming process, and it is expensive. Flooding rinks 24 hours a day means paying overtime for crews. This simply is not cost-effective. So, in Red Wing, there are no longer neighborhood skating rinks all around town. Just one outdoor hockey facility is left because of the economics. Our winters have changed drastically over my lifetime and yours.

Climate change is happening. As individuals and communities we need to find ways to make a difference. The scientific observations match what I am seeing on the ground: that Minnesota's winters are warming faster than any other state in America.

Hockey may have helped shape my entry into my community, but it is not the reason I have stayed. I have spent the last 45 years living in Red Wing, a beautiful city tucked in the bluffs along the mighty Mississippi River. Most citizens here understand that we are responsible for making sure the natural beauty of the surrounding landscape is preserved. There is a realization here that we need to make good decisions today for future generations ahead.

The city of Red Wing has been a leader on environmental issues and as a community has not been afraid to embrace new ideas. In the past decade, the city has been working on solar energy projects, designed to have three parts of equal importance: save money, reduce the city's carbon footprint, and educate others on our process.

I am proud to be part of a community that has a long history of doing what is best for our environment, a history that continues today and, I am sure, will continue well into the future.

For me, the biggest difference I can make is to tell other people how they can help fight climate change. I retired from the city two years ago, but I am still doing my part to fulfill one of the principles of the Red Wing's Solar Energy Projects: education. Being an advisor to Red Wing's Sustainability Commission, speaking to individuals and small business owners through Xcel Energy's Partners in Energy Program, and presenting to various groups about Red Wing's efforts to help reduce greenhouse gas emissions have helped others realize that it can be possible in their community as well.

A long season of outdoor ice will likely never return to southern Minnesota, but if each of us is willing to do our small part, and then partner with others to do even more, we may be able to slow the climate changes that are affecting the places, people, and special aspects of Minnesota that make it our home.

Jay T. McCleary, Age 59
Red Wing, MN
Retired / Minnesotan / Environmental Advocate

Trash Talk

When I was younger, my most significant memories were made outside exploring nature or being intrigued by wildlife. One that stands out most is when my family went to New Mexico and we were hiking on the trails. I was only three years old and was happily running along the trail. I remember feeling the wind on my face and looking out to where the trail cut off and there were bright green trees blowing in the wind. I kept falling down because I wasn't looking where I was going and tripped over tree roots. I got many scrapes but just kept getting back up because I loved it so much.

After many times of this same thing happening that day, my parents gave me the nickname of "trail runner." Because of my curiosity and experiences with nature I have always felt that it should be protected and preserved so that everyone can keep enjoying it.

Up until a few years ago I didn't exactly know what my place was in helping the Earth, but in June 2017, I stumbled upon a YouTube video titled "Four Years of Trash: One Jar," which featured Lauren Singer and her four years' worth of trash in a 16-ounce mason jar. I was completely taken aback and wondered how this was possible. I found out that Lauren lives a zero-waste lifestyle, a philosophy that encourages reuse of almost everything, with a goal of sending no waste to landfills.

To explore this idea further, I watched all her videos which showed zero-waste alternatives to products people use every day that create massive amounts of waste over time. I was inspired. I never realized how unsustainably we live our lives, and how easy it is to make a few changes that greatly reduce the amount of trash we make.

After watching Lauren approach this lifestyle so boldly, I decided to try living zero-waste myself. Many people, including my family at first, were skeptical of this and told me the things I was doing were only a drop in the bucket. But it didn't feel like that to me. Every step that I took gave me confidence. With the help of my dad I dug out a hole in the yard for composting and purchased several alternatives to single-use products; for example, washable bamboo utensils to carry with me instead of using plastic disposable ones. I started using reusable produce bags and reusable shampoo and conditioner containers. I also started buying what I could in bulk and purchased a bamboo toothbrush, compostable floss, toothpaste and deodorant in recyclable packaging.

Anytime I'd do something out of the ordinary I would get interesting looks or questions about why, for example, I dry my hands with a reusable cloth instead of paper towels. I'd tell people who ask that I was trying to live more sustainably and reduce my waste. Instead of feeling judged and uncomfortable in these situations, I took pride in engaging people in conversations about how our society is so accustomed to making massive amounts of unnecessary trash. Even if they didn't take a step for change, having this conversation and seeing someone do something so out of the ordinary made them aware of an issue they may not have seen as an issue before.

I soon realized my more sustainable choices could attract many people's attention and influence others. The most memorable reaction I got was from my sister who is two years older than I. Once I became more conscious of my waste, I started paying attention to others' waste as well. I remember my sister complaining to me when I would remind her what should be recycled because, one, I'm the younger sister and shouldn't be telling her what to do, and two, it annoyed her to be held accountable for her actions. But after a few months passed, she started carrying around bamboo utensils and a metal straw, and is now in college and reminding her roommates what things are recyclable herself.

After a while of being zero-waste, I wanted to take another step for change. I joined my school's environmental club. This was an important step for me because so far I had been doing everything on an individual level, but I always had hopes to change the world. Of course there are steps in between making a lifestyle change and changing the world, and I hoped this would be on step in that process: to spark change in my school or my community.

At one of the club meetings, I learned about the Youth Convening Minnesota project. This project would ultimately bring together the Rochester community to highlight local organizations such as environmental groups and nature centers displaying sustainable options, a 30-minute presentation about the science behind climate change and human causes, personal stories about how climate change has affected people in the community, and solutions workshops to showcase sustainable alternatives. I decided to get involved and was offered the position to be a Youth Core Leader and moderator, and I was ecstatic about this opportunity to engage others about this important issue.

The Youth Convening Minnesota project has built my confidence as a climate leader, and it also allowed me to make connections with other environmental groups in Rochester. Throughout the project, I realized how many people there were who truly cared about climate change and helping the environment, and it gave me hope for a future of sustainability and change.

One thing I've learned is that most people are willing to do the right thing, but often don't realize how they are being impacted by climate change, that our actions matter, and that there are things we can do. For example, before I saw the zero-waste video I didn't realize how much unnecessary trash I made, but after I did, I changed and was mindful of my actions. I hope to continue to prompt people's thinking about climate change just as I am leading by example in my zero-waste efforts, being involved in community outreach, and encouraging others when they ask questions about how to be more eco-friendly.

I want every little kid to experience the curiosity and wonder I had with nature and animals, but with climate change there's no telling how well these animals and the Earth will be preserved. In only 10 years, the year

2030, there could be catastrophic consequences if climate change isn't addressed properly, according to the Intergovernmental Panel on Climate Change (IPCC) report from the United Nations. In 2030, I will be only 29 years old and probably be starting a family of my own.

These climate consequences are well within my lifetime. Slowing climate change will take drastic, unprecedented action, and time is running out. I have confidence that if everyone learns about the severe consequences of climate change, they will be prepared and eager to change to sustainable alternatives, and we can all be a part of addressing climate change together, as one resilient community, to preserve this beautiful planet.

```
Zaria Elisha Romero, Age 19
Rochester, MN
Zero Waste / Concerned Youth / Hispanic
```

For the Earth Warriors...

It used to be that weather was the thing you talked about—
at least in the Midwest—
when there was nothing else to say.
It followed 'Hello' and a mumbled 'How ya doing'
with no expectation of a lengthy reply.

It quickly moved from there to temperatures, wind, or rainfall.
Something you could really sink your teeth into.
It had to do with altered outdoor plans
or rain needed for crops and gardens.
Here in the northland it was about wind chill
and how the old timers used to walk to school
in inclement weather without whining.
That sort of thing.

But these days, talk of weather has changed.
What was once unusual has become the norm.
Hurricanes, droughts, high and low temps—
all are off the charts we've faithfully kept all these years.

Indeed even habitats have changed.
What once supported moose, for example,
has shifted as temperatures climb
expanding the range of deer
bringing parasites and heat stress.

You know this already...or are quickly catching on.
What are we to do with what we know?
At best we feel a dull ache and concern,
other times full on foreboding.

Most of us channel this into action of some kind—
at large or at home, we do what we can
and try to do more.

It's frustrating and terrifying
but there is no temptation to look away.
We feel this in our bones as beings on this planet.
It is a deep inner knowing of something profoundly out of balance.

If this were a pretty poem, it would wrap up now
with something tidy and neat
about how we will find our way.

But this is a gritty poem that knows better.
It joins the chorus of millions upon millions
of voices, hearts and souls
that cry out and will not look away.

So here it is, what I can offer is this...
in your darkest places and times
when your love and actions on behalf of all things Wild
feel not nearly enough,
remember you are not alone.

There are countless like-minded Wild souls here with you
also aware, also not willing to look away.
You can take heart in that.

We are a crafty lot.
And when you need to sigh or cry or fall apart
there are others here to help you pick up the pieces
and begin again. And again.

Until we tilt the circumstances
or die trying.

This beautiful world is worth it.

And you, Earth Warrior, are part of that beauty.

```
Chris Heeter, Age 56
Bloomington, MN
Wilderness Guide / Dogsled Musher / Wild Rice Harvester
```

Communicating our climate stories to elected officials is a powerful way to help move climate solutions at any level of government. The impact of your letter will reflect the care you put in to tell your story.

Who Represents Me?

The District Finder will list your State Senator, State Representative, U.S. Senator, and Congressperson for your address. Try to learn a bit about them to find how climate change connects with issues they tend to focus on.

www.usa.gov/elected-officials

What Should I Write?

- Be concise and thoughtful. Legislators deal with many issues in a short time.
- Grab their attention. Show the impact of climate change in their district using personal stories, examples, or evidence.
- Make the ask. Share a specific action they can take, whether a bill or policy they can influence, and how.

Tips

- Be respectful. Your letter will be more influential if you can find shared values rather than being critical or angry.
- Write clearly. Hand-written letters can be very moving, as long as they are legible..
- Include your name, address, and date. Anonymous letters will be ignored, but by making sure your name and address are there, you may get a response so you can then continue a dialogue and build a relationship.

Climate Generation: A Will Steger Legacy is a collaborative nonprofit in Minneapolis, MN, with a mission to empower individuals and their communities to engage in solutions to climate change.

As a nationally connected and trusted organization, Climate Generation delivers high-quality education, community engagement, and youth leadership programming in Minnesota and the nation.

Proceeds from the sales of *Eyewitness* directly support climate change programming at Climate Generation: A Will Steger Legacy.

Eyewitness was created to communicate Minnesotans' experiences of climate change impacts, and the need for urgent and bold action, to members of the Minnesota Legislature.

To request additional copies of this book please contact Climate Generation:

> Climate Generation
> Email: info@climategen.org
> Phone: 612-278-7147

Learn more about Climate Generation's programs and resources for action on climate change at **www.climategen.org**.

Share your own climate story by submitting to our online storytelling collection at **www.climatestories.org**.